5

Introduction

What do we call the most fearsome and bloodthirsty of the dinosaurs? *Tyrannosaurus rex*. Its name comes from the Greek word 'tyrannos', meaning a ruler who seizes power by force.

Our word 'tyrant' comes from the same source. We use it to describe people who suppress or bully others. They may be kings, queens or presidents ruling an entire country. Or they may be criminals in charge of a gang. They may even be businessmen or religious leaders.

Most tyrants are not elected to power: they just grab it. They do not have the support of the majority of those they rule. They have to keep their positions by force, and by denying human rights.

This book recounts the careers of one hundred famous tyrants. A few of them were monsters, such as the crazy Tsar Ivan the Terrible or Vlad Dracul, who put thousands to death simply to satisfy their mad desires.

Many were monarchs who inherited their position of power, but abused it so that they could keep absolute control of their nation. Among these were Henry VIII of England, Pedro the Cruel of Castile and Catherine the Great of Russia.

However, most of the greatest tyrants have clawed their way to the top through cunning, treachery or violence. Good examples are Adolf Hitler, Mao Zedong or Joseph Stalin, who rose from

100 GREATEST
TYRANTS

Andrew Langley

DRAGON'S WORLD

CHI...

Dra...
Lim...
Sur...
Gre...

Firs...

© 1...

British Library
Cataloguing in Publication Data
The catalogue record for this book is available from the British Library.

ISBN 1 85028 316 8

Editor: Diana Briscoe
Picture Researcher: Josine Meijer
Designer: Mel Raymond
Art Director: John Strange
Design Assistants: Karen Ferguson
                  Victoria Furbisher
DTP Manager: Michael Burgess
Editorial Director: Pippa Rubinstein

Typeset by Dragon's World Ltd
in Stempel Garamond and Gill

Printed in Italy

Contents

humble origins to become dictators controlling the destiny of large parts of the world. Look at Timur Lang or Napoleon I, who built up vast empires in a few years.

Not all tyrants have been power-hungry thugs. Many actually changed their countries for the better by introducing reforms and modern ideas. Genghis Khan allowed freedom of religion and encouraged trade between East and West. Dictators such as Juan Peron of Argentina and Anton Salazar of Portugal encouraged the growth of industry, schools and transport.

Andrew Langley

OPPOSITE
TOP LEFT: Empress Ci-Xi of China.
TOP RIGHT: Mao Zedong and his third wife, Jiang Qing (both featured).
BOTTOM: Emperor Nero of Rome.

RIGHT: Attila the Hun.
BELOW: Tippu Sultan's tiger.

Sennacherib
died 681 BC

▶ This image of Sennacherib on his throne, holding bow and arrows, is from a carving found at Nineveh.

In the seventh century before Christ, the greatest empire in the world belonged to the Assyrians. They lived in the area covered today by northern Iraq. From about 800 BC, Assyrian kings began to conquer the lands to the west, including Syria and Israel.

The most powerful of these rulers was Sennacherib, known as 'the great king, the king of the world, king of kings, prince without rival'. He was the nation's chief priest, and the leader of its army. Much of his fighting was done against Babylonia and Palestine. When the city of Babylon rebelled in 689 BC, he attacked it fiercely and destroyed it. He also destroyed large parts of Palestine and besieged Jerusalem.

Sennacherib left behind him a grand city called Nineveh. Prisoners of war were forced to build him a splendid palace, temples and streets, and two massive city walls nearly 13 km long. The buildings were carved with pictures showing Sennacherib's victories.

▼ The Assyrian forces are given heavenly help in a battle. Ancient Jewish writers believed that Sennacherib was aided by God, because he punished rebels in Israel.

Sennacherib planned to invade Egypt in about 700 BC. But the invasion was stopped – by mice. A plague of them is said to have eaten the bowstrings and arrow quivers of the Assyrian soldiers.

Queen Tamyris

sixth century BC

The king of the Persians, Cyrus the Great, was a mighty and famous man. He conquered many nations in the Near East, and founded a huge empire in the lands previously ruled by the Assyrians (see page 8), which stretched from the Mediterranean to the Hindu Kush. But there was one country he never captured – the land of the Massagetae, a Scythian tribe from the north.

The Massagetae were led by their warrior queen, Tamyris. At first, Cyrus offered to marry her so that he could take over her land. Tamyris scornfully refused. In about 530 BC, she put her son in command of her army and sent him against the invading Persians. When he was killed, she led the troops herself.

The Massagetae, like other Scythian peoples, were fierce horsemen, who rode bareback, firing arrows from their short bows and scalping their dead enemies. They defeated the Persian army. In order to avenge her son, Tamyris ordered that Cyrus should be executed.

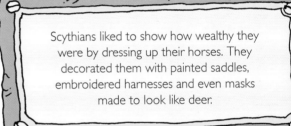

Scythians liked to show how wealthy they were by dressing up their horses. They decorated them with painted saddles, embroidered harnesses and even masks made to look like deer.

▼ This golden comb, found in a barrow grave on the Steppes of Russia, shows Scythian warriors in battle. It dates from the fifth century BC.

Polycrates
died 522 BC

Some people think of Polycrates as the first of the pirate kings. In about 540 BC, he was ruler of Samos, a large island, now belonging to Greece, off the coast of modern Turkey.

He realized that he could become very powerful by building up a strong navy with an army of archers on board the ships. With this, he gained command of the sea and raided other nearby islands. Polycrates became very wealthy and had many beautiful new buildings erected on the island of Samos, including an aqueduct, a temple and a harbour. He kept a grand court, where poets and singers were invited.

Many were alarmed at the power of Polycrates. The king of Egypt warned that even the gods were jealous of him. To save himself, Polycrates was told to throw away something precious, so he threw his favourite ring into the sea. But a few days later, he was given a fish – and inside it was the ring! This was a bad omen! Soon after, Polycrates was captured and murdered by his enemies.

▲ A painting of a trireme in action from a Greek black-figure vase dating from about 500 BC. You can see the huge ram on the prow for holing other ships and the large rudders for steering at the stern.

Most of the ships in Polycrates' war fleet were powered by oars. The biggest ships were triremes, which had three rows of oarsmen, one above the other. The triremes were fitted with a ram at the front, or bow, which smashed into enemy boats.

▼ Samos is blessed with several good natural harbours, which would have made things easier for Polycrates with such a large fleet to house.

Tarquin the Proud
564–505 BC

Tarquin's grandfather was king of Rome. When he was murdered in 579 BC, he was succeeded by a friend, Servius Tullius. When Tarquin grew up, he plotted to seize the throne for himself. When he did this he killed not only Servius Tullius, but also his brother and his wife. Then he married his brother's widow and declared himself the seventh king of Rome.

He was also the last. Tarquin quickly became unpopular – and greatly feared. He put to death all the important citizens who might be his rivals. The greatest scandal was caused by Tarquin's son Sextus, who attacked a noblewoman called Lucretia. The Romans were so shocked by this crime that they rebelled against Tarquin, and he and all his family were expelled from Rome. For the next four hundred years, Rome was a republic – ruled by elected leaders.

▲ This dramatic seventeenth century painting shows the rape of Lucretia by Tarquin's son Sextus. It was also the subject of a long poem by Shakespeare.

▼ Tarquin tries to find out what the future holds by consulting the Sibylline books, a set of prophecies about Rome.

After Tarquin was expelled, the title of 'king' was hated by the Romans. Even when Julius Caesar became absolute ruler of Rome and her territories in 49 BC, he refused to wear a crown or to allow people to call him king.

Shi Huangdi
259–210 BC

At the age of only 13, Zheng Wang became ruler of the north-western state of Qin (old-style Ch'in), the strongest in China. As Zheng grew up, he began to increase its power and sent his armies against the other nearby states. By 221 BC, all of China was under his control. He called himself 'Shi Huangdi', or 'First Sovereign Emperor' and predicted that his family would stay in power for 1,000 generations (about 30,000 years).

The emperor made sure that he would never be threatened by his rivals. All the rich or important families were forced to live in the capital, Xianyang. Roads and canals were built, to make travel easier across the vast area of land that he ruled.

Sections of a wall in the north were joined up to make a barrier against invaders, which is known today as the Great Wall of China.

Shih Huangdi would allow no-one to oppose him. All who disagreed with him were executed. In 213 BC, he ordered the burning of all books (except those on farming, medicine or prophecy). During his last years, he lived inside his vast palaces, never seeing his subjects outside.

Shi Huangdi was buried in a giant grave in a mountain. His body was guarded by over 6, 000 soldiers and horses, all made of clay. This 'terracotta army' was discovered in 1974 and is today a popular tourist attraction.

▼ Part of the army of terracotta soldiers which guards the mausoleum of Shi Huangdi.

Herod the Great
c. 72–4 BC

In 43 BC, Herod was made king of Judaea (now Israel) by the rulers of Rome. But before he could rule his new kingdom, he had to fight hard to defeat his rivals. Once he gained control, Herod began to make Judaea more beautiful. He built magnificent new cities and repaired the Great Temple, the Jews' sacred building, in Jerusalem.

But as Herod grew more powerful, he showed a darker, crueller side to his nature. He ordered an entire family to be killed because he suspected them of plotting against him. Even his own relatives were not safe if he suspected

▲ The Massacre of the Innocents, and the flight of Jesus and his parents into Egypt, are depicted in a French painting from the Middle Ages.

▼ The ghost of Mariamne, executed on her husband Herod's orders, appears before him in a dream. Altogether, he married ten wives, and had fourteen children, including Salome.

Herod's greatest achievements were to repair the Temple in Jerusalem and to construct a splendid new port on the Palestine coast.
He called it Caesarea, in honour of the Roman emperor, Caesar Augustus. It became one of the chief cities of the region.

them. He executed his wife and son, as well as his sister's children.

However, he committed his most bloodthirsty act as he lay dying. He heard that a baby called Jesus had been born in Bethlehem. This child, he was told, would become king of the Jews. Greatly alarmed, Herod ordered his soldiers to search out all the male babies in Bethlehem and put them to death. This slaughter is still known as The Massacre of the Innocents.

Caligula (Gaius Caesar)
AD 12–41

As a boy, Gaius was well liked, especially by the Roman soldiers, who nicknamed him Caligula, or 'little boots'. When he became emperor of Rome in AD 37, cheering crowds greeted him. They were thrilled to have a new leader who was young, clever and generous.

But things changed all too soon. Caligula fell ill, and the disease affected his brain, sending him mad. He began to act in a cruel and vicious manner, and ordered men to be executed for little or no reason. His lions were fed on criminals (who were cheaper than butchers' meat). He ate and drank far too much, and took his sisters as wives.

In his madness, Caligula realized that he had the power to do anything he wished. He even proclaimed that he was a god. This was too much for many of his guards and senators (members of the government). They stabbed him to death after a reign of less than four years.

▲ The head of Caligula stares arrogantly from this aureus, a valuable gold coin issued during his brief and violent reign.

One of Caligula's oddest acts was to build a bridge of boats across the Bay of Baiae – a distance of five km. The boats were lashed together and topped with planks. The emperor proudly drove a chariot over this pointless causeway.

▶ A magnificently dressed Caligula rides Incitatus, his favourite stallion, which he promoted to be a consul (ruler of Rome!). In his left hand, the emperor holds a symbol of a lightning bolt, the weapon of the god Jupiter.

Agrippina
AD 15–59

Agrippina the Younger was closely connected with three Roman emperors. She was sister to the mad Caligula (see page 14) and was mother to Nero (see page 16), through her first marriage. And in AD 49 she became the wife of Claudius (her third marriage), who had become Emperor eight years earlier.

By the time she married him, Claudius was old and weak. Agrippina saw her chance to seize power, and she bullied him into adopting Nero as his successor, and marrying him to Claudius's daughter, Octavia. At the same time she also secretly put all possible rivals to death.

Many noblemen were alarmed that the Empire seemed to be being ruled by a woman. They tried to warn Claudius, but Agrippina was too quick for them. She poisoned her poor husband, and made sure that Nero was proclaimed as emperor.

However, her triumph did not last long. Nero saw that even he was not safe from his mother's lust for power. Agrippina must be killed. But this was not easy. He tried to poison her three times and to drown her – all without success. In the end, Nero sent soldiers to her villa to beat her to death.

▲ A marble head of Agrippina's mother, Agrippina the Elder. She was as power-hungry as her daughter and died in exile, starved to death.

Nero had a special boat made to kill Agrippina. Once out at sea, it collapsed, throwing her into the water. She managed to swim towards the shore, and was rescued by a fishing boat.

▶ This cameo, carved in onyx, depicts two Roman emperors and their wives; on the left, Claudius and Agrippina the Younger; and, on the right, Germanicus and Agrippina the Elder.

Nero
ad 37–68

Nero's father was a violent bully. His mother was Agrippina (see page 15). As his father remarked, any child of this pair was likely to be hateful and dangerous.

So it turned out, after Nero became Roman emperor in AD 54. He poisoned his stepbrother and had his first wife beheaded. He was afraid that people were plotting against him, so dozens of rivals – and followers – were slain. In a fit of temper, he kicked his second wife to death. By AD 64, there was great discontent in Rome. It was made worse when a massive fire destroyed most of the city. Some accused Nero of starting the blaze. He blamed a small sect, the Christians, and had them thrown to his lions. Still the hatred grew, until he was named an enemy of the people. As soldiers came to arrest him, he stabbed himself.

▲ Nero's fondness for rich food and wine made him very fat, as the double-chinned profile on this gold coin clearly shows .

Nero liked to think of himself as a great poet and musician. He loved to recite his verse and play his music in public. During his performances, the doors were locked so that none of the audience could leave.

▼ Nero inspects the ruins after the great fire. He is said to have recited his poetry while watching the city burn.

Domitian

AD 51–96

Domitian had a difficult childhood. He was an awkward, shy boy, and his father (the Emperor Vespasian) did not trust him. All the glory went to his elder brother Titus, who was charming and popular. When Titus became Roman emperor, Domitian dreamed of overthrowing him. Then suddenly, in AD 81, Titus died of a fever. Domitian was Emperor at last. But he distrusted other powerful men around him, especially senators and successful generals. After a rebellion by one of his governors, he began a reign of terror. He built up a network of spies. Suspects were tortured, and important people were put to death for the slightest reason.

Not surprisingly, Domitian was terrified of plots against his life. He shut himself up in his palace and saw as few people as possible. He even had his walls covered with shiny stones, so that he could see anyone creeping up behind him. But early one morning an assassin tricked his way in, and Domitian died.

▼ The last of Domitian's bloodthirsty acts (shown here) was to send assassins to kill his cousin. One of the cousin's servants trapped the emperor in his bedroom and stabbed him to death.

Domitian liked to spend much of the day sitting alone. He passed the time by catching flies and impaling them with a specially sharpened pen. Domitian's children all died in infancy, so the Flavian dynasty ended with his assassination in AD 96.

Attila the Hun

c. AD 406–453

The Huns were a wandering, warlike people from the windswept Asian steppes. They moved westwards and, by AD 433, attacked the borders of the Roman Empire. Their two kings, Attila and his brother, Bleda, led them on raids against the Romans. The Emperor of Constantinople paid them a huge sum of gold each year to avoid these attacks.

Attila decided he wanted success for himself alone. He murdered his brother and became sole king of the Huns. Then he launched savage attacks on the region known as the Balkans. Attila swept ruthlessly on into Italy and later Gaul (an ancient region of western Europe). After causing great devastation, he was at last defeated in Gaul in AD 451. The Huns retreated, but their reputation has lasted until today.

▼ About 1505, the painter Raphael showed Pope Leo X driving Attila's army from Rome by the fear of God. In fact, the Pope paid them not to sack the city.

The Huns plundered vast riches, yet Attila wore plain clothes, and his throne was a simple wooden seat. He died after drinking too much at one of his weddings (he already had about 300 wives). His followers were so upset that they cut their cheeks so they could weep blood instead of tears.

Fredegund
died AD 597

Fredegund worked as a servant at the court of the king of the Franks, Chilperic. She soon caught the king's eye. As his love for her grew, he got rid of his wife Audovera. Then he murdered his second wife, and in AD 568 Fredegund became the new queen.

Already she had many enemies. The most dangerous was Brunhilda, the sister of the murdered queen. With her husband, Sigebert, Brunhilda started a war against Chilperic. It was a bitter struggle, during which Fredegund showed how ruthless and heartless she could be. She plotted Sigebert's murder, then she had her own stepchildren put to death. Then, in AD 584, Chilperic himself was mysteriously killed.

▶ The historian Gregory of Tours, whose biased account of Fredegund's life fixed her reputation as a cruel and ruthless woman.

Fredegund's greatest success was to make sure that her son, Lothair, eventually became king of the Franks. Unlike his mother, Lothair was a wise monarch, who managed to end the long civil war in France.

No-one knows if Fredegund was to blame. All the same, she seized her husband's wealth and fled to Paris. Here, she carried on her fight for power, and finally defeated Brunhilda in AD 597. However, Fredegund did not enjoy her success, for she died soon afterwards.

◀ Brunhilda later became a central figure in a German epic poem, and is a major character in Wagner's opera cycle, The Ring of the Nibelung.

Wu Zhao

AD 625–705

As a young girl, Wu Zhao (old-style Wu Chao) was very beautiful and was chosen to be one of the many wives of the first Tang emperor of China, Taizong (T'ai-tsung). When he died, Wu Zhao quickly began to gain power. She became the favourite wife of the new emperor, Gaozong (Kao-tsung). She had her rivals killed (including other wives) – by AD 655 she was empress of China.

Gaozong was weak and ill. Seizing her chance, Wu Zhao took over the running of the state. When Gaozong died, the empress refused to give up her power to the new emperor – her own son, Zhongzong (Chung-tsung). She ordered him into exile and took the throne for herself. For the first time, China was ruled by a woman.

Though Wu Zhao was ruthless, she was also a fine ruler. Her reign brought

▲ A statue of a court lady of the Tang period, found in a grave. There are no portraits of Wu Zhao.

▼ This beautiful Dancing Horse was made during Wu Zhao's reign. It was put in a tomb so that its owner could ride it in the afterlife.

peace to China and victory over Korea. She chose her own officials, and did not care if they were from rich or important families. After nearly fifty years of power, she was at last forced to abdicate by Zhongzong. She retired to her summer palace at the age of 80.

Long after Wu Zhao's death, Chinese writers described her as no more than a cruel tyrant. They could not accept that a woman might make a good monarch. More recently, however, her achievements have been praised.

Harun-al-Rashid

AD 763–809

In AD 800, Baghdad was one of the most magnificent cities in the world. It was the capital of the Islamic empire. Ruled by the mighty caliph, Harun-al-Rashid, the city was inhabited by scholars, wealthy traders, fine craftsmen, and artists from many lands.

Harun-al-Rashid was a generous man, who encouraged these people to make Baghdad even greater. But he also had a cruel side to his nature. In AD 803, he became jealous of one of the most important families in the city, the Barmecides, and ordered that they should all be killed. Harun-al-Rashid

▼ A later illustration from *The Arabian Nights*, a huge collection of folk stories from Egypt, Persia (Iran) and China, featuring beautiful peris (fairies) and wicked djinns (demons) and magicians.

Harun-al-Rashid sent many wonderful gifts to Charlemagne, king of the Franks. Among his presents were an elephant and a water clock, which marked the hours by dropping bronze balls into a bowl, while mechanical knights appeared through doors.

also led his armies in several wars against the Christian Empire at Byzantium, and eventually died in battle.

Many legends have sprung up about Harun-al-Rashid and he appears in *The Arabian Nights*. In one story, he disguises himself as a poor traveller and walks through the streets of Baghdad at night. He is in search of adventures, and wants to learn the true feelings of his subjects. In another, he commands a magician to make him a pair of spectacles that will allow him to identify honest men.

Eadburga
ninth century AD

Eadburga was one of the daughters of Offa of Mercia. He was one of the greatest of Anglo-Saxon kings, and built up an empire stretching across southern England. As part of his plans, he married Eadburga to Beorhtric, King of Wessex (one of his territories), in AD 789.

Eadburga soon became a notable figure at court, scheming and plotting to gain more power for her husband. But her plots ended in disaster. In AD 802, she attempted to poison one of her rivals. Beorhtric drank the poison by mistake, and died.

Eadburga quickly gathered as much wealth as she could carry, and fled to the protection of the Holy Roman Emperor Charlemagne, in France. Once again, she managed to plot her way to a position of influence. But her behaviour shocked many in the French court, and she was expelled. It is thought that she died in Italy, alone and in poverty.

▼ The Emperor Charlemagne, shown here inspecting progress, built a magnificent church and palace for his court at Aachen, Eadburga must have seen much of the construction process.

Eadburga's murderous ways brought shame on all the later wives of the kings of Wessex. They were no longer called 'Queen', but were addressed as 'The Lady' instead.

Saint Olga

AD 890–969

How can someone be both a saint and a tyrant? Olga's story is strange and surprising. She was a ferry girl near Moscow, rowing people across the river. One day, she had a royal passenger – Prince Igor of Muscovy (the area around Moscow in present-day Russia). He was so struck by her beauty that he gave her a valuable ring. Later on, Olga married Igor and became the Grand Princess of Russia.

In AD 945, Igor was murdered by rebels, and Olga became regent for her son who was still a child. She was the first-ever female ruler of Russia. When she had gained power, she took an appalling revenge on the rebels. Their leaders were scalded to death, and hundreds of others were executed.

In AD 957, she became a Christian, and was baptized in Constantinople. She tried to convert many other Russians to Christianity. After her death, she became the first Russian saint.

▶ Olga encouraged the spread of the Orthodox form of Christianity throughout Russia. Saints in the Orthodox Church were depicted in richly-coloured paintings called icons.

In spite of Olga's efforts, Christianity did not spread in Russia while she was alive. Her son, the new ruler, would not allow it. But her grandson, Vladimir, turned Russia into a Christian country in the 990s. He, too, was made a saint.

Alfgifu
c. 995–c. 1040

Alfgifu came from a noble family in Northampton. Her great beauty quickly impressed England's new king, the young Cnut. Cnut, already ruler of Denmark, had conquered England in 1016. Alfgifu became his mistress, and bore him two sons. Swein, the eldest, was made king of Norway, and in 1030 Cnut sent her to rule there as regent. She ruled so severely and brutally that the Norwegians rebelled against her, and she was driven out.

Alfgifu was determined that her second son, Harold Harefoot, should be

▲ A miniature portrait of King Cnut, from an illuminated manuscript made in the early Middle Ages.

the next English king. But there were many others who could claim the throne. When Cnut died in 1035, Alfgifu moved swiftly. She forced the rest of the nobles to accept Harold as temporary king. Then she helped plot the murder of his nearest rival. With the other claimants abroad, no-one could oppose Harold, who became full king of England in 1037.

Harold Harefoot reigned for only four years before his death. He was succeeded by Cnut's legitimate son, Harthacnut, who ordered Harold's body to be dug up and thrown into a bog.

◀ Queen Alfgifu (bottom left) and king Cnut (bottom right) place a cross on the altar of Newminster and Hyde Abbey, Winchester.

Genghis Khan
c. 1167–1227

In 1206, a chieftain of the Mongols from central Asia called together all the local tribes. He demanded that they should make him their leader. They hailed him as 'Genghis Khan', or 'Ruler of the World', for the first time uniting the Mongols under one emperor.

Genghis Khan's army was huge. By 1218, it had invaded China. Then he swept westwards through Persia (now Iran), plundering and burning great cities. At Bokhara, Genghis himself led the attack, shouting to the terrified enemy that he was the 'Flail of God' come to punish them. Meanwhile, he sent another army into Russia. Genghis Khan built up the biggest empire the world had ever seen. But on yet another expedition he caught a fever and died.

▲ Genghis Khan sits majestically in his yurt – a type of felt tent used by the Mongols.

▼ This European print shows Genghis Khan being shot with an arrow - an entirely imaginary event, for he died in bed!

Sometimes, Genghis Khan ordered that everyone in a captured city should be put to death. He knew that news of the massacre would travel faster than his armies. When he reached the next city, the citizens would be so terrified that they would surrender without a fight.

Pedro the Cruel
1334–69

Pedro was only 15 years old when he became king of Castile in Spain. He was in love with a beautiful girl called Maria, but politics prevented him from marrying her. The king of France wanted Pedro as an ally in his struggle against England, so Pedro's family forced him to marry Blanche of France. Pedro hated his new wife, and soon deserted her (some say he even murdered her). Maria remained his mistress for the rest of his life.

Pedro was now an enemy of France. He also angered the Pope, by refusing to visit him. Worst of all, he faced rebellion from his four half-brothers. He had three killed, but the fourth, Henry, escaped to France. With the help of the French, and mercenary troops, Henry drove Pedro out of Castile. Pedro himself looked for support, and persuaded the English to help him win back his throne and the bitter civil war went on.

▲ Like his father King Alfonso, Pedro tried to establish a strong monarchy in Castile. This angered the Castilian nobles, who rebelled against him.

According to legend, Pedro and Henry met in single combat. Yelling their war cries, they hacked at each other with axes until Pedro was overcome. However, it is more likely that he was simply betrayed and handed over to his half-brother.

▼ The murder of Pedro at the hands of his half-brother Henry, as imagined by a nineteenth-century artist.

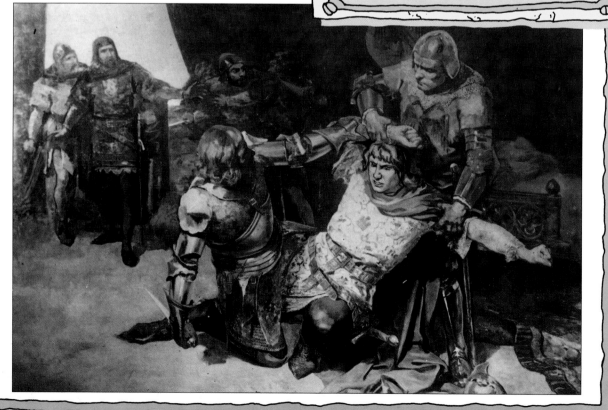

Timur Lang
1336–1405

Timur was born with a crippled right leg (in the Mongol language his name means 'the lame'). But his leg was no handicap, and he became a fine athlete and warrior. He believed that he was descended from Genghis Khan (see page 25), and was determined to rebuild the huge empire of the Mongols.

Even as a young man, Timur began to seize control of the tribes near his birthplace, Samarkand. By 1369, he was the sole ruler of the region. Within ten years, his armies had conquered all of Persia. He thundered on, crushing the Russians and Tatars. Then he invaded northern India and sacked the great city of Delhi.

Timur was just as savage as Genghis Khan. In 1387, the people of Isfahan in southern Persia (now Iran) rose in revolt and killed many of his soldiers. Timur ordered a horrifying revenge. All 70, 000 citizens of Isfahan were executed, and their heads piled in vast pyramids outside the city walls. However, unlike Genghis Khan, Timur was a bad ruler. As soon as he died, his empire fell apart.

▶ Timur's bloodthirsty rise to power was dramatized by English playwright Christopher Marlowe in his massive two-part tragedy of 1590 called *Tamburlaine*.

Timur wanted to make Samarkand into the finest city of the East. He ordered beautiful new homes and temples to be built. But even in this he was ruthless. If he disliked a building, he had the architect beheaded.

Bernabo Visconti
1309–85

The terrible Visconti family ruled two Italian cities: Galeazzo Visconti, lord of Pavia, was a fearsome ruler, but his brother Bernabo, of Milan, was a monster. When he rode through its streets, everyone had to kneel. Those who disobeyed or annoyed Bernabo were savagely punished. He had devised a programme of torture which lasted forty days (the programme was published, just to frighten the citizens).

Bernabo's wild behaviour and hunger for power alarmed his nephew, now ruler of Pavia. He devised a clever plan to capture Bernabo. Pretending to be on a pilgrimage, he invited Bernabo to meet him outside the walls of Milan. There he had him seized and flung in a dungeon. Bernabo died a few months later, probably poisoned.

▲ After murdering his uncle, Bernabo of Milan, Gian Galeazzo Visconti conquered many cities, and became ruler of most of Northern Italy.

▼ Bernabo Visconti receives envoys from the Pope, whom he regarded as his servant, outside Milan.

The Visconti family rose to power in 1262 when Ottone Visconti became Archbishop of Milan. Their emblem was a snake, which was swallowing a human figure. The snake was a symbol of cunning.

Tomas de Torquemada

1420–98

Tomas de Torquemada was a man with a mission. As a Spanish friar, he believed completely in the teachings of the Roman Catholic Church. No-one was allowed to question them, and any Christian who did so was a heretic.

Torquemada was convinced that heretics were a threat to Spain. Non-Christians, such as Jews and Muslims, were an even greater danger. He thought that they should all be hunted down and punished.

The Pope in Rome already had a system of dealing with heretics. Called the Inquisition, it was a ruthless investigation into the activities of those who questioned the Church. Now Torquemada persuaded the Spanish king, Ferdinand, to establish the Inquisition in Spain, and he became its stern leader, the Inquisitor-General, in 1483. Torquemada encouraged King Ferdinand to get rid of the Jews in Spain. The king was already jealous of their success and wealth. In 1492, he passed an edict expelling over 160,000 Jews from the country.

Under Torquemada, the Spanish Inquisition grew into a frightening and powerful force. People suspected of heresy could be tortured until they were forced to confess. If they returned to strict Catholic beliefs, they might be lightly punished. But if they refused, they would be executed. During Torquemada's period as Inquisitor-General, over 2,000 heretics were burned at the stake.

The Inquisition was first established in southern France in the thirteenth century by the Order of Dominicans to try and persuade a group of heretics, known as the Cathars, of the error of their ways. Ironically, torture was forbidden to begin with – reason only was to be used.

◀ The horrors of the Court of the Inquisition are shown graphically in this mural by the twentieth-century Mexican painter Diego Rivera.

Vlad Dracula
1431–76

This is the story of the real Count Dracula. His name was Vlad Tepes, and in 1456 he became ruler of Wallachia (in present-day Romania). One man who met him described Vlad as 'very stocky and strong, with a cold and terrible appearance'.

Vlad's reign was one of the most terrible and cruel in history. He had at least 50,000 people put to death – about one-tenth of Wallachia's population. One day he invited all the country's beggars to a feast. Then he had the building set on fire, burning them all to death. When some Italian diplomats refused to take their caps off to him, he ordered his servants to nail the caps to their heads. However, Vlad's favourite way of killing people was to impale

▲ It is easy to see how this pale bloodshot portrait inspired later writers to link Vlad with legends of vampires.

Vlad was not in fact a vampire, or drinker of blood. But his nickname Dracula, meaning 'The Dragon' or 'The Devil', was used for the undead, blood-sucking count in Bram Stoker's novel of 1897, and has since become a household name.

them on sharpened stakes. During a war against Wallachia, the Turkish sultan attacked Vlad's castle. Along the route, he passed some 20,000 stakes, each with a dead and rotting Turkish corpse.

When the Turks finally defeated Vlad, they had their revenge by placing his head on a pole and displaying it high above the city of Constantinople (now Istanbul in Turkey).

◄ This castle, the birthplace of Vlad Tepes, is in present-day Romania. It looks an ideal setting for the home of the fictitious Count Dracula.

Pope Alexander VI
1431–1503

Rodrigo Borgia was a very clever man. He was also lucky. His uncle was the Pope, and made sure that Rodrigo rose quickly in the Roman Catholic Church. He became a cardinal, and grew rich and powerful. But he did not live a holy life for, although he was fat, bald and rather ugly, he had many mistresses and several illegitimate children.

In 1492, Rodrigo was elected as Pope (he paid rewards to those who voted for him), and took the name Alexander VI (after Alexander the Great). He had reached the top, but his first concern was to make sure that his children also became wealthy and gained power.

His favourite son was Cesare, a subtle and clever soldier. Alexander appointed him as archbishop, then as cardinal and finally as a duke. When Alexander died suddenly, Cesare was imprisoned.

▲ Alexander made his family extremely wealthy by gaining power over the local Italian princes and seizing hold of their riches. Using the money of the Church, he tried to make Cesare king of central Italy.

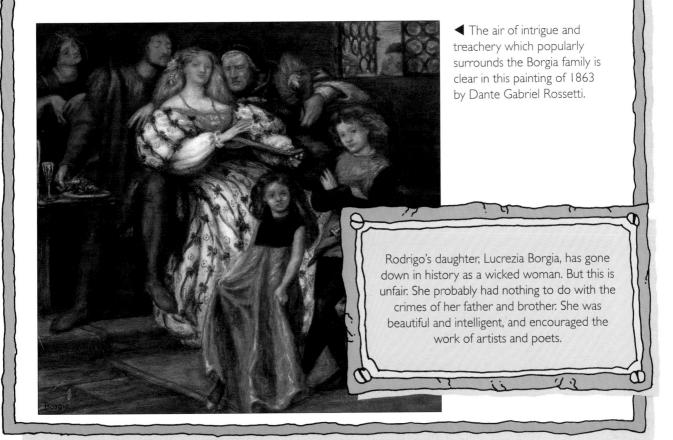

◄ The air of intrigue and treachery which popularly surrounds the Borgia family is clear in this painting of 1863 by Dante Gabriel Rossetti.

Rodrigo's daughter, Lucrezia Borgia, has gone down in history as a wicked woman. But this is unfair. She probably had nothing to do with the crimes of her father and brother. She was beautiful and intelligent, and encouraged the work of artists and poets.

Richard III
1452–85

Richard, Duke of Gloucester thought he would never be king of England. His elder brother became King Edward IV in 1461. In 1483, the crown passed to his son, Edward V, but the new king was only a boy of 12. Richard was named as Lord Protector to rule. The widowed queen disliked and distrusted Richard. She and her family tried to seize control, but Richard defeated them. He imprisoned or executed all the noblemen who opposed him.

He shut Edward and his brother in the Tower of London, and the two young princes disappeared. Crowned king, Richard soon became unpopular. In 1485, Henry Tudor led an invasion against him. They met in battle at Bosworth where Richard was killed.

▲ Richard's reputation was blackened by many later writers to strengthen the position of the Tudors.

Swift action by Richard made Edward V's reign one of the shortest ever. Edward had been king for only 78 days when his uncle seized the throne and locked him in the Tower of London. Some say that Richard ordered their murders, though this has never been proved.

▼ Richard's nephews, the 'Princes in the Tower'. Bones found two centuries later were presumed to be theirs, and were re-buried in Westminster Abbey.

Francisco Pizarro
1474–1541

Pizarro was born in Spain, and was later abandoned by his parents. He became a swineherd and then a soldier. In about 1502, he joined an expedition to the Caribbean island of Haiti. From here he travelled to Panama and seemed to be no more than a tough, quiet settler.

Then, in 1523, Pizarro began exploring the west coast of South America. He heard tales of the wealthy Inca people of Peru and determined to find them. Backed by the Spanish king, he set sail with a ship and only 180 men. They arrived in Peru in 1532, to be faced by the Inca emperor, Atahualpa, and an army of 30,000 soldiers.

Although heavily outnumbered, Pizarro did not

Atahualpa promised to pay a huge ransom – he would fill an entire room with gold and another two rooms with silver – in return for his release. He kept his promise, but was not released. The treasure in the three rooms would be worth over £30 million today.

retreat. The Inca soldiers were so frightened by the Spaniards' guns that they retreated and Pizarro was able to capture Atahualpa and murder him. Pizarro now had Peru at his mercy. His men sacked the great Inca treasures and sent them home to Spain. The entire Inca empire was destroyed. Pizarro himself was killed by Spanish rivals in 1541.

◀ This precious gold female idol is an example of the type of Inca treasure Pizarro and his men plundered as they captured Peru.

42 IDOL: female figure of thick sheet gold with extended arms. Face bears traces of green paint.
CULTURE: INCA

Henry VIII
1491–1547

When Henry became King of England in 1509, he seemed an ideal monarch. He was handsome, energetic, and a fine fighter. He wrote music and spoke several languages. But there was one thing he desperately wanted – a son to be king after him.

Henry's wife, Catherine, failed to produce a male heir to the throne, and so he sought to divorce her and re-marry. At the time, England was a Catholic country, which obeyed the orders of the Pope in Rome. The Pope would not allow Henry to divorce. Defiantly, Henry married a new wife, Anne Boleyn, in secret. He then broke England's links with Rome and declared himself head of the English church.

This caused uproar, but Henry went even further. He closed down all the Catholic monasteries and seized their wealth. He crushed anyone who opposed him, imprisoning or beheading them. In old age, he grew fat and ill, but he still terrified his courtiers. Few dared to argue with him.

▲ Henry surrounded by his six wives. From the top, clockwise, they are Anne of Cleves, Catherine Howard, Anne Boleyn, Catherine of Aragon, Catherine Parr and Jane Seymour.

▼ Although he looks majestic in this grand painting of 1541, Henry was by this time getting very fat and suffering from crippling pains in his legs.

Henry had six wives altogether in his search for an heir. He divorced two, and two were beheaded for treason (but actually because they were supposed to have found lovers). One died of disease, while the last outlived him. Three children also survived. They became King Edward VI, Queen Mary I and Queen Elizabeth I.

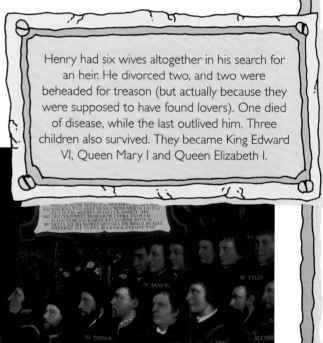

Catherine de Medici

1519–89

Two tragedies struck Catherine in two years. First her husband, King Henry II of France, was killed in an accident in 1558. Then, in 1560, her eldest son, Francis II, also died. The new king was her 10-year old son, Charles. Catherine was made Regent, to rule the country until Charles grew up.

At this time, two religious groups were struggling for power in France. On one side were the Catholics, backed by Spain. On the other were the Protestants, led by a group called the Huguenots. Catherine tried with all her cunning and energy to keep them from fighting each other, but in vain. After three civil wars, Catherine became desperate. In 1572, she ordered the killing of over 4,000 Huguenots in Paris. This was known as the Massacre of St Bartholomew's Day, and shocked the whole of Europe. Catherine's power was never so great afterwards.

▲ Catherine with her two youngest sons, Charles and Henri. Her eldest son Francis was married to Mary, Queen of Scots, but died very young in 1560.

▼ Huguenot men, women and children are slaughtered by Catholics during the St Bartholomew's Day Massacre in Paris, 1572.

Catherine was actually an Italian by birth. She was a member of the great family of Medici, which ruled Florence for over 200 years, and turned it into the magnificent city it is today.

Ivan the Terrible
1530–84

Ivan grew up in the royal court of Russia. He lived in terror of the brutal and reactionary noblemen, or boyars, whom he knew were plotting against his life. At only 17, he was crowned emperor, or tsar, of Russia. Now, suddenly, he was free to do exactly what he liked. This mixture of fear and limitless power unbalanced his mind.

When his beloved first wife died in 1560, Ivan plunged further into madness. He began a campaign against the boyars, killing them without trial. He set up a secret police force whose members dressed in black and carried a severed dog's head as their symbol. On Ivan's orders, they massacred the 60,000

▼ Despite his awful reputation, Ivan reformed Russian law and encouraged learning. This page comes from one of the many illustrated chronicles compiled during his reign.

▲ A modern impression of Ivan and his deeds by a twentieth-century Russian artist, I. Glazunov.

Ivan married no fewer than eight times. In 1567, he even proposed himself as husband to the English Queen Elizabeth I. This match would have made him King of England. Fortunately, Elizabeth refused him.

citizens of Novgorod in 1570. In the same year, there were mass public executions in Moscow. Ivan grew increasingly vicious and bloodthirsty. In a violent fit of rage, he killed his own son. This shocked him so deeply that he never slept properly again, but roamed the palace at night in terrible remorse.

Ieyasu Tokugawa
1543–1616

In the 1590s, most of Japan was controlled by the powerful general, Hideyoshi. Ieyasu Tokugawa was warlord in a small fishing village called Edo. He supported the general, but he also began building a large castle, and strengthening his army. When Hideyoshi died in 1598, Ieyasu marched out with his army and defeated rival warlords to take control of Japan. Soon he was made military leader, or shogun, of all Japan.

Next, Ieyasu made sure that he and his sons would never be threatened. Edo was turned into a stronghold. Thousands of men laboured to enlarge the castle until it was the biggest in the world. Anyone who might lead a rebellion was forced to live nearby, as a hostage. In 1614, Ieyasu destroyed the remaining members of the Hideyoshi clan – his last enemies.

Ieyasu transformed Edo from a village into a busy town. In 1868, it was given a new name, Tokyo, and became the new capital of Japan. It is now one of the largest cities in the world. The Tokugawa family remained in command of Japan for the next 250 years.

▼ Matsumoto (Nine Cranes) Castle in Nagano-ken, Japan. This must have been much what Ieyasu's castle looked like when new.

Boris Godunov
1551–1605

Boris began his career under Ivan the Terrible (see page 36), and learned some of his master's cruel methods. After Ivan's death, Boris schemed his way into a post with great power. He used Ivan's secret police to spread terror. Other noblemen were tortured, imprisoned, executed or sent into exile. Ivan's last son, Dmitri, was mysteriously stabbed to death.

In 1598 Boris himself was crowned tsar. But bad harvests caused famine and disease, which killed thousands of people. Boris's bloodthirsty behaviour had also made him many enemies. A man claiming to be Dmitri gathered a Polish army and invaded Russia. When Boris died, he left Russia to suffer many years of civil war.

▲ Under Boris, education and the arts flourished in Russia. This beautiful altar cloth dates from 1601.

▼ When Tsar Fyodor died in 1598, he left no heir to the Russian throne. The priests and noblemen begged Boris to become the new ruler.

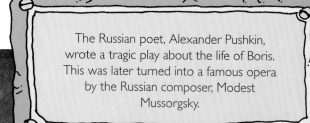

The Russian poet, Alexander Pushkin, wrote a tragic play about the life of Boris. This was later turned into a famous opera by the Russian composer, Modest Mussorgsky.

Countess Elizabeth Bathory
1560–1614

Elizabeth Bathory was born into a powerful Hungarian family of princes and soldiers. Her beauty made her famous, and at 16 she married a local count. But, as her husband was a soldier, and often away at war, she grew bored.

At first, she found a lover. Then she began to brood on old age. Terrified that she would lose her looks, she believed that her beauty could be preserved by bathing in the blood of virgins. Over 600 young girls were lured to her castle, butchered and drained of blood. In 1610, one of the girls escaped and brought help.

Elizabeth's helpers were put to death, but she was spared because she came from an important family. Instead, she was bricked up in her castle. Her only contact with the outside world was through a tiny slit in the wall.

▲ Elizabeth Bathory has been known as the 'Bloody Countess' since 1610.

▼ The traditional way to destroy a vampire was to drive a stake through his or her heart. Often then the body was burnt and the ashes scattered at a crossroads outside the town or village.

By a strange coincidence, Bathory's great-uncle, Stephen, was an ally of Vlad Dracula the Impaler (see page 30). Vlad was the original inspiration for the Dracula legend as told by Bram Stoker in his famous novel *Count Dracula*.

Jahangir
1569–1627

Jahangir's father was Akbar the Great, third Mogul emperor of India, one of the great rulers in history. Jahangir found it difficult to follow his father's example, and grew up lazy and cruel. He drank too much and smoked a strong drug called opium. He even rebelled against his father. Even so, Akbar named him the next emperor.

Jahangir tried to carry on as his father had done. He fought wars against rival princes, but he was too idle to take on the daily governing of his empire. He handed this over to his wife, Nur Jahan, and spent his time building palaces and gardens. He also paid artists to paint many beautiful pictures in the Persian style. Drink and drugs made Jahangir steadily more violent. He ordered many suspected enemies to be tortured or put to death. But as he lost control, there were frequent rebellions. In 1626, Jahangir was captured by rebels. He died a year later.

▼ One of Jahangir's enemies, Gosain Narayan, is forced to drink poison while the Emperor looks on.

For all his cruelty, Jahangir did not force anyone to follow his own religion (he was a Muslim). He even allowed Catholic missionaries to hold debates at his court with Islamic scholars.

Nur Jahan
1571–1634

Mehr on-Nesa was a beautiful Persian woman. She was brought up in India, and gained a post at the royal court. Here she met the Emperor Jahangir (see page 40), who fell in love with her. She became his chief wife in 1611, and took the title of Nur Jahan.

Jahangir was a lazy man, who was addicted to alcohol and the drug opium. Soon, Nur Jahan began to have great influence over him. She made her brother the chief minister, and married her niece to a member of the royal family. By the 1620s, the emperor had handed over most of his power to her.

▲ Mogul hunters kill a tiger with their spears. This picture was painted on cotton.

Jahangir's son, Shah Jahan, became the new emperor. He married Nur Jahan's niece, Mumtaz Mahal, but she died young. The heartbroken Jahan erected a great tomb of white marble in her memory. It is one of the world's best-loved buildings – the Taj Mahal.

Nur Jahan revelled in her strong position. She issued coins, played polo and hunted tigers. But her arrogant ways upset many people, including Jahangir's son, Khurram, who rebelled against her. After Jahangir died in 1627, Khurram seized power and Nur Jahan was forced to retire into the harem.

◀ The Taj Mahal at Agra, built between 1632 and 1653.

Aurangzeb
1618–1707

For nearly half a century, Aurangzeb was the ruler of the huge area that is now India and Pakistan. He had reached this position by imprisoning the emperor (his father), Shah Jahan, and by killing three of his brothers.

Aurangzeb was a fervent Muslim (a follower of the Islamic faith) and discouraged other religions. He forced all non-Muslims to pay a special tax. In 1675, Aurangzeb put to death a Sikh leader, who was the father of the last Sikh Guru, Govind Singh, for refusing to become a Muslim. This began a feud between Sikhs and Muslims which lasted for centuries. There were also rebellions by Hindus.

As time went by, Aurangzeb's religious laws grew more and more strict. Hindu shrines and temples were destroyed. Words of Muslim scripture were removed from coins, so that they could not be touched by non-believers, or infidels. Works of art were broken up in case they were worshipped as idols. The anger and uprisings caused by these laws made India a weak and divided country.

Aurangzeb had seized power by rebelling against his father, Shah Jahan (see box on page 41) when Jahan fell ill in 1657, He also executed two of his brothers. But in 1680, his third son, Akbar, led a rising of the warlike Rajput tribes of the north against Aurangzeb. This was easily put down.

▼ Aurangzeb examines the head of his brother Dara, whom he had executed after defeating him in battle in 1658.

Frederick William I

1688–1740

When Frederick William became king of Prussia in 1713, he had only one interest in life – his army. He wanted his troops to be the toughest and best disciplined in Europe. His court was run like an army barracks, and anyone who disobeyed orders or broke his rules was severely punished, including his son and heir.

The most treasured part of William's army was his personal Prussian Guard. These soldiers had to be the tallest in Europe. To get tall men, he even had suitable recruits kidnapped from their homes. Members of the guard were encouraged to marry tall women, so that they could produce suitably tall children.

William spared no effort in building up army numbers. Peasants were forced to join up. Even the sons of noblemen could not escape, and were trained as officers. Soon the Prussian army was strong and perfectly organized. However, the king was so proud of it that he hated the idea of spoiling it with warfare. He did his best to avoid battles.

▲ Frederick William scorned such things as poetry and philosophy, and spent most of his great energy in soldiering. He was known as the 'Soldier King'.

Frederick William did sometimes attend to other matters. besides the army. His most valuable ruling was to make schooling compulsory for young Prussian children. His son, Frederick the Great, was an intellectual as well as a solder.

▼ Frederick William goes stag hunting with his pack of hounds.

Nadir Shah
1688–1747

Nadir began his career as a bandit chieftain in Persia (now Iran). He was so inspiring a leader that he soon became the country's military chief. Driving his armies on, he defeated the Turks and scared the Russians into surrender. By 1736, he had made himself Persia's sole ruler, or shah. He continued his conquests by invading northern India and sacking the great city of Delhi, where he massacred thousands. He returned home with fabulous treasures, including the Peacock Throne and the Koh-i-noor diamond.

By now, Nadir's ruthless cruelty had grown almost to madness. He continued to fight pointless wars, causing enormous bloodshed. When he suspected his eldest son of treachery, he ordered him to be blinded. In the end his own soldiers murdered him in disgust.

Nadir Shah loved warfare so much that he was horrified when he learned that paradise was a peaceful place. 'How then,' he asked, 'can there be any delights there?'

▼ The Peacock Throne can be seen behind the last Shah of Persia, Mohammed Reza, during his coronation ceremony. Here he has just crowned Farah Diba, his wife.

Mary Read 1690–1720 & Anne Bonny died 1720

Mary Read's mother used to dress her in boy's clothes. When Read grew up, she liked to dress as a man, and worked first as an inn servant, then in the navy and then as a soldier in the army. After many adventures, she found herself on board a ship which was captured by pirates. The pirates were led by Jack Rackham and a woman pirate, Anne Bonny.

Bonny also dressed in men's clothes and was the most feared fighter in the crew. She and Read quickly became close friends, and the leaders of the pirates. Together, they attacked treasure ships in the Caribbean. In one battle, the male pirates hid below in fright. Read shouted at them to come out and fight, and shot those who disobeyed her order.

Their adventure ended in 1720, when

▲ Brandishing a cutlass, Mary Read is shown in a romantic and dashing pose.

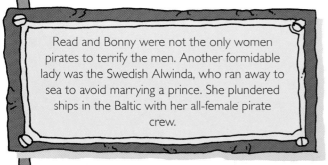

Read and Bonny were not the only women pirates to terrify the men. Another formidable lady was the Swedish Alwinda, who ran away to sea to avoid marrying a prince. She plundered ships in the Baltic with her all-female pirate crew.

their ship was captured by the British navy. The men were hanged, but the women were spared because they were pregnant. Mary Read died of fever in prison, but no-one knows what happened to Anne Bonny.

Edward 'Blackbeard' Teach

c. 1680–1718

As 'Blackbeard', Edward Teach was the most famous and feared of all pirates. He looked terrifying. His long black beard was plaited with ribbons, lighted fuse cords hung from his hair surrounding him with clouds of smoke, and across his chest were strapped six pistols.

Blackbeard raged up and down the east coast of the USA, looting cargo ships and even attacking boats in harbours. Anyone who was unwilling to give up a ring had his finger chopped off. Teach wanted to scare not only his victims, but also his crew. He kept them in order with great savagery, even shooting his first mate in the knee, so as 'to remind his crew who he was'.

This ferocious pirate was eventually cornered by a ship of the British navy. He fought a desperate battle with Lt Robert Maynard, and died with twenty cutlass wounds and five bullets in him. Maynard cut off his head and hung it from a mast in triumph.

Blackbeard was actually born in Bristol, England, and fought for the British against France and Spain before becoming an outlaw. Many legends and tall stories have been told about Blackbeard since his death. He was even the hero of a play in 1798, in which he rescued an Indian princess.

▼ Blackbeard's last fight. Many believe that he had hidden a hoard of treasure, and that the secret of its location died with him.

Catherine II the Great
1729–96

At only 16, Catherine left her Prussian home to become the wife of the young tsar, Peter III of Russia. But she soon grew to hate her weak and stupid husband and, helped by her lover, removed Peter from the throne.

In 1762 she made herself empress, and arranged for Peter to be quietly murdered soon afterwards. Catherine was a brilliant and hard-working monarch. She made many reforms in Russia, building new schools, urging women to become educated, and improving health care. She encouraged artists and writers to come to Russia, and even abolished the death penalty (except for treason).

However, many Russians were still very poor and unhappy. Catherine did nothing to help the huge class of serfs who worked the land and were little better than slaves. In 1774 there was an uprising against her, led by a man who pretended to be her dead husband, Peter. The revolt was savagely crushed, and whole villages burned to the ground in revenge. After this, Catherine turned her back on reform, and became a harsh and repressive ruler.

▲ The Empress Catherine was notorious throughout Europe because of her liking for young and handsome guardsmen. One, Grigori Potemkin (above), conquered much of what is now southern Russia for Catherine and acquired a huge fortune in doing so.

In 1787, Catherine toured southern Russia. This was a poor and backward region, but her then-lover (Prince Potemkin) had smart new villages built along her route, to persuade her that everyone was prosperous and happy. These were known as 'Potemkin villages'.

◀ The Empress Catherine in a very masculine pose on horseback. Nearly all women wore skirts and rode sidesaddle at this time.

Tippu Sultan
1749–99

Tippu's father was the Muslim ruler of Mysore in India. At the time, most of India was dominated by two European powers, Britain and France. Tippu learned to support the French (who taught him how to lead troops) and hate the British. When he became sultan himself in 1782, he first of all made peace with Britain.

However, he could not contain his hatred, and in 1789 he invaded one of their territories. This was disastrous, for he was eventually defeated and lost half of his own lands. Tippu had always been a cruel and fanatical man, but this failure made him more violent still. All captured enemies were tortured and brutally killed. Tippu continued to plot against the British in India. At last, in 1799, the British lost patience and launched an attack on his capital at Seringapatam. Tippu died in the fighting.

▼ This is Tippu's notorious toy, which can now be seen in the Victoria and Albert Museum in London, England.

Tippu's hatred of Britain was so great that he had a mechanical model made of a tiger eating an Englishman dressed in a uniform of the East India Company.
Run by clockwork, the model makes a sinister growling noise as the tiger savages its victim.

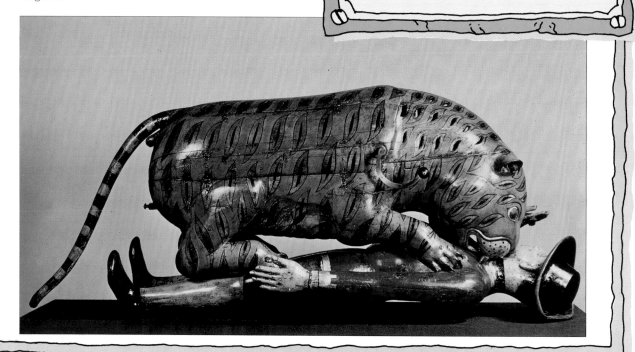

Tsar Paul I
1754–1801

Paul had an unhappy childhood. His mother (later Catherine the Great, see page 47) despised his father, Tsar Peter III, and had him murdered. When Paul grew up, he reminded Catherine so much of her dead husband that she hated him too. He was not given any position of power until she eventually died in 1796. Paul then became the new tsar of Russia.

Paul was an unstable ruler. He tried to reverse his mother's laws, and had the body of one of her lovers dug up and thrown on to a rubbish heap. He also put limits on the power of the nobles. Anyone who disobeyed him might be flogged, branded with hot irons and have their noses slit. The final straw was when he entered into a close alliance with Napoleon Bonaparte in 1801, after having been a firm supporter of the Allied Coalition against Napoleon previously.

Angry and alarmed, the nobles decided that Paul was too insane to reign. Supported by the British, they plotted to depose him. In 1801, they burst into the tsar's palace and ordered him to give up the throne. When he refused, they strangled him with a scarf and battered him to death with a stone paperweight.

▲ As a young man, Paul was sent away to a remote estate in the countryside. Here he formed a private army, which he delighted in training himself.

Paul wanted to make his army as strong and efficient as the Prussian one. He made himself very unpopular with his troops by forcing them to wear stiff, uncomfortable Prussian uniforms instead of their old, softer ones.

Joseph Fouché
1759–1820

When France suffered a Revolution in 1789, cunning men had their chance to gain power. One of the most clever of these was Joseph Fouché. For over twenty years he switched sides, supporting whoever was leading the country. In 1793, he was sent to punish the people of Lyons for refusing to support the Revolution. Fouché ordered hundreds to be beheaded by the guillotine or shot. But soon afterwards he gave his support to those who condemned such violence.

Fouché became minister of police in 1799, and supported France's new leader, Napoleon (see page 51). He organized a secret police force, with a network of spies and bullies. By 1807 he believed that Napoleon would soon be overthrown and began plotting with his enemies, the British. Napoleon dismissed him.

▲ In 1815, Fouché made friends with the new King of France's government, and was appointed minister of police yet again. But he was soon revealed as a traitor and sent finally into exile.

Even as a student, Fouché had changed sides. He was trained to be a priest at colleges in Paris and Nantes, but quickly turned against the church. He became one of the leaders of the Revolution's new Godless religion, and organized a 'festival of reason'.

▼ Marie Antoinette, Queen of France, is executed by the guillotine during the Revolution in 1793.

Napoleon Bonaparte
1769–1821

Napoleon Bonaparte is one of the most famous men in history. Although he was not very tall (only 1.5 m), he eventually became emperor of France and built a huge empire in Europe. He was a brilliant general with a ruthless thirst for power.

During 1796, at the height of the French Revolution, the young Napoleon was put in command of the army in Italy. After conquering northern Italy, he swept on into Egypt. In 1799, he returned home and within a few months had become dictator. Napoleon worked hard to reorganize France, creating a new system of laws.

In 1804, he crowned himself emperor. He had close control of the newspapers and the police, and kept a network of spies to inform on possible traitors, but the French people grew tired of his dictatorship. In 1815, he was finally defeated at Waterloo. He was sent into exile on St Helena.

Napoleon's invasion of Russia was one of the greatest military disasters in history. Although he captured Moscow, he was then forced to retreat through the bitter winter. About 500,000 of his 600,000 soldiers died or were captured during the campaign.

▼ Napoleon crowns Josephine as his Empress at a sumptuous ceremony in 1804. By now, his lust for power and glory had alarmed many supporters.

Jingshi
c. 1780–c. 1820

In the early 1800s, the most feared pirate in the China Seas was Jingyi. But in 1807 he and his ship disappeared in a hurricane. His pirate empire was taken over by his widow, Jingshi. She turned out to be an even more savage fighter than her husband.

Jingshi commanded an enormous fleet of pirate ships – over 1,800 in all, sailed by 80,000 men and women. With this, she attacked cargo vessels and naval ships up and down the Chinese coast.

With such a massive force, she needed to keep strict control. She compiled a list of orders for her crews, and anyone who went ashore without permission had his or her eardrums punctured. All captured valuables had to be shared out equally.

Jingshi spread terror wherever she sailed, burning whole villages and massacring the inhabitants. But in 1810, after quarrels with her captains, she surrendered to the Chinese government. Amazingly, she was not put to death, but carried on her shady activities – as a smuggler!

Jingshi boasted to her pirates that she would pay them extra for every head they brought her. They carried them two at a time, with the pigtails knotted together, slung around their necks.

▼ Naval ships were not immune from pirate attack. Here Chinese pirates attack Lieutenant Turner and a boat's crew from the British ship HMS *Tea*.

Agustin de Iturbide
1783–1824

In the early 1800s, Mexico was in the midst of a revolution to overthrow the Spanish rulers. The rebel leader needed good generals for his army, and offered a post to Agustin de Iturbide, an experienced officer. Iturbide refused – he supported the Spanish king instead.

By 1820 the revolution had failed. Amazingly, Iturbide now joined forces with the one remaining rebel leader. Within a year, their army had taken over the country, and Mexico had won its independence from Spain.

However, Iturbide was a very ambitious man, who believed that Mexico should be ruled by a king. His allies disagreed, and wanted Mexico to be a republic (led by a president and an elected government).

In 1822, Iturbide seized power and, imitating his hero Napoleon, crowned himself as Agustin I, emperor of Mexico. But he was a hopeless ruler and was soon forced to flee the country. When he returned in 1824, he was captured and shot.

After Iturbide's fall, Mexico quickly became a republic, whose people could elect their own president and government. But more trouble lay ahead (see page 62).

▼ Mexico has had a turbulent history ever since it overthrew the Spanish overlords. This fresco by Diego Riviera shows many of the principal contestants.

Ludwig I
1786–1868

King Ludwig was an extravagant man. He spent a fortune on turning the Bavarian capital, Munich, into a grand centre for the arts. He paid for many splendid buildings and collected fine paintings.

Not surprisingly, the Bavarian people saw this as a terrible waste of money. But Ludwig did not care – he believed that Bavaria's money was his to spend as he wanted. Then, at the age of 60, he fell madly in love with an Irish-born dancer called Lola Montez. In 1847, Ludwig forced his ministers to make her a countess, and lavished gifts on her.

▲ Ludwig's obsession with Lola Montez nearly brought revolution to Bavaria. After the affair, the dancer travelled to the USA and joined the California Gold Rush of 1849.

Ludwig's son and successor, Ludwig II, was even stranger than Ludwig I. His obsession was for building fantastic-looking castles and for the music of Richard Wagner. In 1886, the increasingly insane king was drowned in a lake – it was probably suicide.

This caused riots in Munich, led by students, which were quelled by the army. Ludwig closed the university. In 1848, however, revolution was in the air all over Europe, and the rioting grew worse. Under great pressure, the king first of all banished Montez, and then gave up the throne.

◀ Neuschwanstein (New Swan Castle), one of the many fantastic castles built by Ludwig I and his insane successor, Ludwig II.

Shaka Zulu
1787–1828

Shaka was the son of a Zulu chieftain in southern Africa. Separated from his father in childhood, he grew into a courageous warrior. When his father died in 1816, Shaka became the new chieftain.

At the time, the Zulu were one of the smallest and weakest of the local clans. Shaka began building them into the strongest. He reorganized the army, dividing the soldiers into regiments, and training them. With this force he crushed the neighbouring clans and joined them to the Zulu. Within eight years, the Zulu nation had grown from 1,500 to over 50,000 people.

Shaka had always been cruel, but when his mother died in 1827 he went insane with grief. On his orders, 7,000 Zulus were put to death, and no crops were planted. Soon his half-brothers could stand no more, and murdered him.

▼ In 1824, a British trading party, led by a naval officer, visited Shaka and persuaded him to sell a large portion of territory to the British Crown.

▼ A modern day Zulu impi performs a traditional war dance in South Africa.

Shaka turned the Zulu nation from wandering cattle herders into fearsome warriors with a huge empire. His terrifying army, or impi, could travel 80 km each day, carrying their assegais (short stabbing spears) and oxhide shields. A band of boys carried the impi's sleeping mats and other equipment. Food was taken from the tribes in the areas that the Zulus passed through.

Juan Manuel de Rosas
1793–1877

Rosas was born to a wealthy family of cattle ranchers on the Argentinian grassland, or pampas. As a young man, he built up his own estates, and gathered an army of gauchos (cowboys) which he used to fight against the local Indians. Soon he became a powerful figure.

Rosas was appointed governor of the Buenos Aires region in 1829. His term only lasted three years, but his strong leadership made him very popular. In 1835, he was asked to become governor again. Rosas agreed, as long as he was given the power of a dictator. He remained in supreme command of the region for seventeen years, crushing all opponents with his troops and secret police force. No-one dared to argue with him. Rosas even ordered that his portrait should be placed in churches and public squares.

Rosas' power was ended by a joint army from Brazil and Uruguay, which defeated him in battle near Buenos Aires in 1852. He fled to Southampton, England, where he lived quietly until his death.

During the career of Rosas, Argentina, although independent of Spain since 1816, was made up of separate regions. It did not unite as a single country until 1862, when Buenos Aires became the national capital.

◀ The gauchos, or cowboys, of Argentina were as wild and lawless as those of the American West. Several times they were important in installing political regimes in Argentina.

Nicholas I
1796–1855

Nicholas was the son of the mad tsar, Paul (see page 49). No wonder then that he grew into one of the harshest of all Russian rulers. Tall, stern and handsome, he worked unceasingly to stop revolution in his empire. Nicholas succeeded in 1825 after his elder brother, Alexander, died. He immediately took complete control of newspapers, books and universities. He created a secret police force to prevent any plots against him. A rebellion in Poland (then part of the Russian empire) in 1830 was crushed with great violence by his armies.

Nicholas also fought in Asia, but when he tried to attack Turkey, he found himself up against the armies of Britain and France. The result was the Crimean War (1854–6). The war was a disaster for Russia, and Nicholas died a disappointed man before its end.

▲ Nicholas was given a broad and rigorous education, including a tour of England in 1817.

▼ The British Light Brigade make their disastrous charge at Balaclava in 1854, during the Crimean War.

Queen Victoria was impressed and disturbed by the tsar. 'His profile is beautiful,' she wrote, 'but the expression of the eyes is unlike anything I ever saw before. His mind is an uncivilized one.'

Ferdinand II
1810–59

Ferdinand's father, the king of Naples and then Sicily, had hated the French and their revolutionary ideas. He ruled as an absolute monarch, allowing no-one to question his decisions. When Ferdinand became king of Sicily in 1830, he seemed a much more liberal ruler. He freed political prisoners and began to reform the government.

But this did not last and Ferdinand soon became worse than his father. Even so, he could not stop the revolution sweeping Italy in 1848. He was forced to allow a government to be elected in Sicily for the first time. A few weeks later, encouraged by a victory over the rebels, he once more took charge of Sicily after a savage bombing campaign and ruled it as a tyrant until his death.

▲ Seated lovingly with his family at the Bay of Naples, Ferdinand does not look like a tyrant.

Ferdinand's shelling of the Sicilian cities in 1848 was so ferocious that he was nicknamed 'King Bomba'. It also earned him the hatred of many European leaders. Meanwhile, the other Italian states had unified, leaving Sicily alone. Soon after Ferdinand's death, the island became part of Italy.

▼ Some of the men led by Giuseppe Garibaldi, who conquered Sicily and Naples in 1860 in his attempt to unite the different kingdoms of Italy.

Hong Xiuquan
1814–64

Hong was a clever child, and his very poor parents hoped he would pass an examination to become a civil servant. But he failed the test again and again. Then Hong dreamed that an old man gave him a sword, and told him to get rid of the evil spirits in the world. Convinced that the old man was God, Hong decided that he must therefore be a Son of God sent to save China.

In 1851, he proclaimed himself as 'Heavenly King' and began to plan a rebellion against the Qing rulers of China. Soon he had an army of more than a million people, called Taipings.

In 1853, the Taipings captured the great city Nanjing (Nanking) and killed many of the inhabitants. But then Hong seemed to go mad, murdering his senior officers and refusing to defend the city – God, he said, would look after his Son.

▲ Taiping officers and soldiers in Nanjing. All the insurgents were native Chinese rebelling against their foreign Qing emperor and his nobles.

The Taiping rebellion was one of the most bloodthirsty in history. Over twenty million people are thought to have been killed during its fourteen years. More than 100,000 of them were slaughtered by Qing (Manchu) troops after the recapture of Nanjing. This happened only seven weeks after Hong committed suicide because he was seriously ill.

▼ The Taipings open fire on the *Lee* gun-boat.

Theodore II
c. 1818–68

A hundred and fifty years ago, Ethiopia was split up into many provinces, ruled by bandit kings who argued and fought with each other. With courage and great leadership, Ras Kassa united the provinces, and in 1855 declared himself emperor of Ethiopia. He took the name Tewodros, or Theodore.

At first, the new emperor carried out many reforms, such as ending slavery and paying his soldiers properly. He was also friendly towards the British. When a British engineer was killed, Theodore attacked the culprits and slaughtered them. But the friendship with the British quickly turned sour. Theodore wrote a letter to Queen Victoria and received no reply. Angry and insulted, he imprisoned British officials and missionaries, and began torturing and killing his own followers.

In 1868 a British force arrived to rescue the prisoners, defeating Theodore at Magdala. The emperor shot himself three days later, with a pistol given to him some years before by Queen Victoria.

▼ The corpse of Emperor Theodore being viewed by British army officers in Magdala in April 1868.

One of Theodore's most lasting achievements was to introduce a style of white baggy trousers to his country. Ethiopians still wear them today.

Antonio Guzman Blanco

1829–99

In 1821, Venezuela was one of the first South American countries to win its independence from Spanish rule. However, it did not stay free for long. After many years of civil war, the country was ruled by a series of dictators, or caudillos. The most powerful of these was Antonio Guzman Blanco.

As a member of the liberal side in the civil war, Guzman was in favour of progress and reform. In 1870, he seized control of Venezuela, and was elected president three years later. However, all too soon he became anything but liberal. His opponents were imprisoned or murdered, the newspapers were strictly controlled, and little was done to help the poor.

Guzman's dictatorship lasted for nineteen years. During that time he used his position to build up enormous wealth, and took many holidays in Europe. This led to his downfall. While he was abroad in 1889, a revolution at home overthrew him. He spent his last years as an exile in Paris.

The name Venezuela means 'Little Venice' in Spanish. The first explorers to arrive there in the 1500s thought Indian coastal villages looked like the Italian city of Venice.

▲ As dictator, Guzman did much to modernize Venezuela. He ordered the building of roads, schools and railways, and curbed the power of the Catholic Church.

Porfirio Diaz
1830–1915

When he was a teenager, Porfirio Diaz trained as a Catholic priest. But when war broke out between Mexico and the USA in 1846, Diaz became a soldier and proved to be a brilliant leader. When peace returned, he went back to his home in Oaxaca.

Before long, Diaz was in revolt against the Mexican president. His rising failed, and he fled to the USA. In 1876, he tried again, and defeated the president's army. He was quickly elected as president himself, and was to remain as dictator for the next thirty-four years.

Diaz was a strong ruler, using his well-organized army to keep control. He also had many powerful friends who supported him – in return he helped them to grow very rich. Mexico, too, became wealthier, as mines and oil wells were developed, and railways were built. However, most Mexicans remained very poor, as much of the money went to landowners and businessmen. Unrest increased until, in 1911, Diaz was forced to resign.

▼ Most of Mexico's new industries, such as oil and mining, were developed by foreigners. As a result, most of the profits went abroad.

Porfirio Diaz was born a mestizo – meaning that he was half Spanish and half native Indian. As president, he won the support of other mestizos by giving them good jobs.

Ci-Xi
(old style Tz'u-hsi), 1835–1908

For more than fifty years, one woman held China in her grip. Ci-Xi was the wife of an emperor, the mother of a second, the aunt of a third and the great-aunt of a fourth.

Ci-Xi had her beauty to thank for the start of her amazing career. She was chosen to be one of the wives of the Emperor Xianfeng (Hsien-feng), and bore his only son, Tongzhi (T'ung-chih). When Xianfeng died, the boy was only 6 years old, so Ci-Xi ruled as regent in his place. But Tongzhi died young (some say his mother plotted his death), to be replaced by his cousin Guangxu (Kuang-hsu).

The new emperor started a programme of reform. This horrified Ci-Xi, who wanted no changes in the ancient Chinese way of government. Backed by crooked friends,

▲ A rather idealized portrait of the Dowager Empress, published in a French magazine in 1900. At this time, she was 65 years old.

Ci-Xi's full title was, 'Motherly Auspicious Orthodox Heaven-Blessed Prosperous All-Nourishing Brightly-Manifest Calm Sedate Perfect Long-Lived Respectful Reverend Worshipful Illustrious Exalted Empress Dowager'! Her nickname within the Forbidden City was 'The Old Buddha'!

she overthrew Guangxu, imprisoned him and ruled in his name. She quashed all reforms, and encouraged a bloody uprising (the Boxer Rebellion) against the hated foreigners in China. Thanks to her, China remained a backward and weak nation.

◄ Russian sailors and civilian defenders repelling an attack by the Boxers in Beijing in October, 1900.

Henry Morton Stanley
1841–1904

Today, Stanley is famous as the man who found the Scottish explorer and missionary, Dr David Livingstone, in central Africa. But Stanley was also known as Bula Matari, the 'Smasher of Rocks' who let nothing – and nobody – get in his way. He was a great explorer, who proved that Lake Victoria was the source of the River Nile. Yet he was also a brutal leader, who drove his men on with beatings and threats.

Stanley made three expeditions to the heart of Africa. The first, in 1871, was to find Livingstone. The second, in 1875, lasted for 999 days and ended with an epic journey down the River Congo. The third, in 1886, was a mission to rescue the governor of southern Sudan. Each journey was an exhausting and terrible adventure. Yet Stanley survived them all. He was certainly a tyrant, but without him the expeditions might have ended in disaster.

▲ The famous meeting – Stanley was too overcome to say more than 'Dr Livingstone, I presume?'

▼ With kicks, whippings and harsh words, Stanley pushed his followers to the limit. He also ordered the shooting of any Africans who got in his way.

Stanley's real name was John Rowlands. But he never knew his father, and was abandoned by his Welsh mother. He emigrated to the USA, where he was adopted by a rich merchant, called Henry Stanley.

Mutesa, Kabaka of Buganda
1838–84

Mutesa was every inch a king. Tall and slim, he had piercing eyes and large, white teeth. All his subjects had to grovel before him. When he walked, he stiffened his legs like a lion. When he sat, a page crouched behind him to act as a living chair.

Mutesa ruled Buganda (part of present-day Uganda) by fear and cruelty, just as his ancestors had done. Every day, people were tortured or burned alive, even for minor offences such as talking too loudly. When a British explorer presented him with a rifle, Mutesa handed it to a servant and ordered him to go out and shoot somebody – anybody – to test the weapon.

Under Mutesa, Buganda grew strong by raiding neighbouring tribes and seizing their wealth. He even had a navy of war canoes controlling Lake Victoria. He was also open to new ideas, and welcomed European traders and missionaries.

It was usual for Central African rulers to start their reign with a shocking massacre, so that their subjects would be terrified. When Mutesa came to the throne, he had sixty of his brothers burned alive.

▼ The approach to Mengo, the capital of Buganda, drawn by Stanley in *Through the Dark Continent* (1878). Inset is another portrait of King Mutesa.

Victoriano Huerta
1854–1916

In 1913, Mexico was ruled by the kind and popular President Francisco Madero. But the rich and powerful Mexican landowners wanted to get rid of him. They gave their support to Victoriano Huerta, a tough soldier who led Mexico's army. On 18 February, Huerta overthrew Madero and had him shot (officially 'while trying to escape').

Huerta immediately established himself as Mexico's dictator. He used his troops to crush all opposition, and abolished the Parliament. Within a few weeks, he had made many enemies. Freedom fighters, led by men such as Pancho Villa and Emiliano Zapata, struggled against him, while the USA demanded that he resign.

When US soldiers stormed the port of Veracruz, Huerta fled first to Spain and then to the USA, where he was arrested and charged with plotting against Mexico. He died in prison.

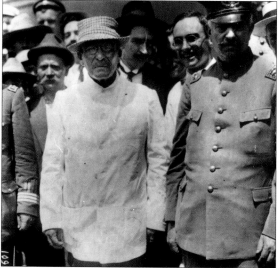

▲ Huerta (left) was so unpopular as dictator that his reign lasted for only seventeen months before he was forced to flee into exile.

Even after Huerta's fall, Villa and Zapata (shown below with some of their troops) fought against the Mexican government – and the Americans. In 1916, Villa crossed the border and raided Columbus, in New Mexico. He is still a national hero today.

William Randolph Hearst

1863–1951

Hearst's father was a millionaire who owned a gold mine and a newspaper, the *San Francisco Examiner*. Hearst took control of the struggling paper in 1887, and quickly turned it into a huge success by filling the pages with large headlines, sensational stories and lavish pictures.

His newspaper empire grew rapidly. By 1925, he owned twenty-five journals covering almost all the USA. He tried many tactics to sell more copies than his rivals. He cut prices, ran promotions and concentrated on gruesome reports of murder and scandal. This became known as 'yellow journalism'.

Hearst hated foreigners, and through lies and wild demands, he urged readers to support a war between the USA and Spain in 1898. His power over public opinion was enormous.

▲ Hearst with his mistress Marion Davies at a Military Ball. He promoted her career as an actress by giving her starring roles in his films.

Hearst's life was the inspiration for one of the most famous of all films, Orson Welles' *Citizen Kane*. Made in 1941, it shows Kane as a power-crazy monster. Hearst, naturally, hated the film and tried to have it banned.

Juan Vicente Gomez
1864–1935

Born in a remote mountain region of Venezuela, Juan Gomez had little schooling. But he became a powerful figure in the area, and began to build up a huge fortune. At the time, Venezuela was torn by civil wars. Gomez joined the rebel army led by Cipriano Castro, and in 1899 helped him to capture the capital, Caracas, and seize power. For this, he was appointed vice-president.

But Gomez had a greater ambition – when Castro was overseas in 1908, he overthrew him and became president himself. Until his death, Gomez ruled Venezuela with a grip of iron. He kept order with his powerful army, and used agents to spy on his rivals. He bought up estates and businesses throughout the land. However, he also brought great riches to Venezuela by selling oil drilling rights to US and European companies.

▲ It is difficult to tell from this grand photograph that Gomez was born an almost full-blooded Indian and had little schooling.

Oil was first discovered in Venezuela in 1918, near Lake Maracaibo. It is now the country's most important industry by far, accounting for 80 per cent of export earnings.

▼The riches from oil helped Venezuela to pay off all her debts to foreign governments.

Miguel Primo de Rivera

1870–1930

Primo de Rivera's father was a governor-general, and Miguel spent his youth at a military college in Toledo in Spain. As a young officer, he saw action in many parts of Spain's overseas empire.

In 1922, he was appointed as captain general of Barcelona. At this time, the Spanish government had grown very weak, undermined by anarchy and rebellion. The king saw Primo de Rivera as a strong leader, and begged him to seize power. So, in 1923, he became dictator of Spain. He suspended the Cortes (Parliament), used the army to enforce his power and also took control of newspapers. He made the papers print an appeal to all Spaniards to be loyal to 'Country, Religion and Monarchy'. Despite all his efforts, he grew more and more unpopular. In 1930, even the army turned against him, and he resigned.

▲ Primo de Rivera with his generals during the Spanish campaign in Morocco in 1924. His victory there was a popular success.

In 1933, Primo de Rivera's son founded the Falange, Spain's fascist party, in imitation of Hitler and Mussolini. Although he was captured and executed early in the Spanish Civil War, the Falange itself was taken to power by Franco (see page 77).

▼ Spain lost the last remains of her American empire during the war of 1898. Here, US troops man trenches near Manila in the Philippines.

Syngman Rhee
1875–1965

In 1910, Syngman Rhee returned home to Korea from his studies in the USA. To his horror, he found that the country had been taken over by the Japanese. Rhee wanted Korea to be independent of Japan, and immediately went back to the USA to campaign for the cause. He was elected president of the government in exile. After Japan's defeat in 1945, Korea at last gained freedom, but at a price. It was split into North and South zones. Rhee was rewarded by being made president of South Korea.

When Kim Il-Sung's Communists invaded from North Korea in 1950, he asked the United Nations for help. The result was a long, bloody and futile war. However, Rhee's supreme power was never in doubt. He had opposition leaders murdered or imprisoned, controlled elections and made sure only his supporters became mayors and village headmen. But by 1960, the South Koreans were sick of his corrupt methods and forced him to resign.

Rhee had an amazingly wide education. After going to a traditional Chinese school, he learned English at a Christian college. Later, he went to Princeton University, USA, where he became the first Korean to qualify as a Doctor of Philosophy.

▼ Exhausted refugees from the Korean War sit by the roadside as an American army convoy moves towards the front to face North Korean invaders in 1950.

Joseph Stalin
1879–1953

Stalin was expelled from college at the age of 20 for belonging to a secret group which wanted a communist revolution in Russia. He went on organizing strikes and demonstrations, and was imprisoned many times. Then, in 1917, Russian revolutionaries forced the tsar from his throne. Cunning and ruthless, Stalin slowly made himself one of the strongest figures in the Bolshevik party who ended up in power.

When Lenin, the Bolshevik leader, died in 1924, Stalin took his place and got rid of all possible rivals. By the 1930s, Stalin was dictator of Russia. Anyone who opposed him was sent to a labour camp. Millions starved to death after he took all farms into state ownership. Everyone feared arrest and torture by his secret police. No one dared to criticize him until after his death.

▼ Thousands of opponents were sent to harsh labour camps such as this one in Siberia. The camps were part of the GULAG, a name which stood for 'Main Organization of Corrective Labour Camps'.

Stalin's real name was Joseph Dugashvili. He changed it in 1912 to Stalin, which means 'man of steel'. This was in imitation of Lenin, who had also changed his name (Lenin means 'man of iron').

Benito Mussolini
1883–1945

By 1919, the communist revolution had triumphed in Russia. Rich Italians feared the same thing might happen there, and they looked to one man to save them – Benito Mussolini. With their money, he founded the Fascist Party and promised to recapture the glories of Ancient Rome. Mussolini made stirring speeches and struck dramatic poses. His followers called him Il Duce ('Leader').

By 1922, Mussolini was so strong that he led a march to Rome to demand power. The king was so frightened that he asked him to become prime minister. Mussolini rapidly made himself Italy's dictator, and banned all other political parties. But after Italy was invaded by British and US forces in 1943, Italian partisans shot Mussolini and hung his corpse upside down in a Milan square.

▲ Mussolini, in swaggering pose, makes a speech in 1928, surrounded by other Italian Fascist leaders. They are wearing their famous black shirts.

Mussolini started a programme of public works to give Fascism a good image. He built motorways, drained marshes and improved rail services. He tried to build up an empire by invading Ethiopia in 1935, and took Germany's side in the Second World War.

▼ Mussolini (left) joined a Fascist alliance with Adolf Hitler (right) called the Axis. Italy and Germany later made a "Pact of Steel" in 1939.

Adolf Hitler

1889–1945

Hitler is the most famous tyrant of all. Dictator of Germany for twelve years, he ordered the death and imprisonment of millions of innocent people. He provoked the Second World War (1939–45), causing millions more to die.

In 1922, Hitler and his National Socialist (Nazi) Party promised to make Germany powerful again after losing the First World War (1914–18). With his spellbinding speeches and brilliant organization, Hitler was in complete control of Germany by 1934. His opponents were sent to concentration camps, Jews and others were persecuted, and the armed forces grew rapidly.

In 1936, Hitler began to build his Third Reich, taking over Austria and Czechoslovakia. By 1939, Germany already ruled much of Europe. After four terrible years the war swung against Germany, and by 1945 the Allies were victorious. Hitler ordered that his body should be burned, then killed himself.

▲ Hitler gives the Fascist salute at a march-past of troops in Leipzig in 1933.

Hitler's most appalling crime was to order the extermination of European Jews, known as the Holocaust. They were rounded up, taken to death camps and slaughtered. Over six million Jews died in this way, as well as huge numbers of gypsies, gays and Slavs.

▼ More than 12 million people died in concentration camps such as this one at Auschwitz. The prisoners were shot, gassed, starved or simply worked to death.

Antonio Salazar
1889–1970

Stern, quiet and thrifty, Salazar was a single-minded man. Some even called him dull. As a university professor of economics, he had very definite views on how to get Portugal out of its financial crisis in 1926. But when he was offered the post of minister of finance, he refused it, saying he would not have enough control.

Two years later, things were so bad that Dr Salazar's demands were met, and he joined the Portuguese government.

This was the beginning of his steady rise to power.

He became prime minister in 1932, and gave Portugal a new political system, partly based on the fascist ideas of Hitler. It abolished press freedom, among other things, and ensured that everyone in the National Assembly (the Parliament) supported Salazar's government.

Though firmly in control, Salazar ruled without fuss or show. He kept Portugal neutral during the Second World War. He encouraged the modernization of the country's railways, roads and shipping, and built new schools in country areas. In 1968, after years of hard work, he became ill and was forced to leave office. However, his refusal to grant freedom to Portugal's African colonies left a legacy of colonial wars in Angola and Mozambique that are only now being resolved.

After Salazar's death, Portugal slowly became a more liberal and democratic country again. There was an army coup in 1974 which led to the introduction of a new constitution in 1975. Its first free elections for over half a century took place in 1976.

◀ Although he stayed in charge of Portugal for so long, Salazar lived a simple life, never once going abroad. He hated the limelight, and rarely appeared in public.

Rafael Trujillo
1891–1961

In 1918, US troops were stationed in the Dominican Republic to keep the peace, and to train local soldiers. Among their most promising pupils was Rafael Trujillo, who quickly rose to command the police force, and then was made a general. During a military rising in 1930, Trujillo seized power and became president. He immediately made sure that he would stay at the top. Members of his family were given important government jobs, and the army murdered Trujillo's main opponents.

Though he was a tyrant, Trujillo was also an efficient ruler, bringing peace and prosperity to the Republic. But his savage methods alarmed foreign governments, and rebels at home began to plot his death. He survived several attempts on his life, but in 1961 was mown down in a hail of machine-gun bullets. The remaining members of his family soon fled the country.

▲ Trujillo with a grandson in 1960.

The Dominican Republic's territory (along with modern-day Haiti) is on one of the islands visited by Christopher Columbus during his voyage of 1492. He christened it 'Hispaniola' or 'Little Spain'.

▼ This is the car in which Trujillo was assassinated. There were more than sixty bullet holes. in it.

Arthur Seyss-Inquart
1892–1946

As a young lawyer in Vienna, Seyss-Inquart had one great dream – to see Austria united with Germany. In this, he agreed with Hitler (see page 73). When Hitler became dictator of Germany in 1934, Austria was the first country he decided to invade. Meanwhile, Seyss-Inquart had risen to become leader of the Austrian Nazis. He kept in close touch with Hitler and his ministers, and helped to cause the fall of Austria's Chancellor Schuschnigg in 1938. After that, it was a simple matter to become chancellor himself and welcome the arrival of German troops.

With Austria firmly under German control, Seyss-Inquart found other ways of serving the Nazi cause. In 1940, he was appointed Commissioner of the occupied Netherlands, where he ruled with great brutality – Jews were rounded up and sent to death camps; resistance suspects were tortured and executed.

▲ After Germany's defeat, Seyss-Inquart was found guilty of war crimes and hanged.

▼ 'This is a photo as I would wish myself to look all the time. Then I would maybe have a chance to come to Hollywood' – the poignant words of young Anne Frank, who hid from Nazi forces in Amsterdam until betrayed and sent to a death camp.

Dit is een foto, zoals ik me zou wensen, altijd zo te zijn. Dan had ik nog wel een kans om naar Holywood te komen.

Anne Frank.

Among the Jews who went into hiding in the wartime Netherlands was Anne Frank. Anne and her family were eventually betrayed and sent to a concentration camp. There Anne died of typhus, but the diary of her ordeal is still read all over the world.

Francisco Franco
1892–1975

A soldier of great promise, Franco was promoted to general in Spain's army at only 34. Franco had right-wing ideals, and supported the monarchy, so he was shocked when, in 1931, Spain became a republic, and the king left the country.

The new government was left-wing. Many Spaniards were alarmed at its liberal ideas, and in 1936 a revolt began. This turned into a civil war. Franco took charge of the anti-government forces, the Nationalists. After much bitter fighting, the Nationalists were victorious in 1939, and Franco became dictator.

During the Second World War, Spain under Franco did not fight, but gave help to Hitler and Mussolini. After the war, he remained firmly in command, limiting personal freedom and controlling the press. As he grew older, there were increasing protests at his rule from students, workers and rebels in the region known as the Basque country.

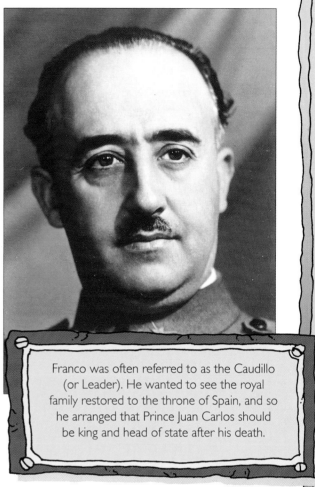

Franco was often referred to as the Caudillo (or Leader). He wanted to see the royal family restored to the throne of Spain, and so he arranged that Prince Juan Carlos should be king and head of state after his death.

▼ Loyalist (government) supporters man a barricade in Barcelona during the Spanish Civil War.

Johannes Strijdom
1893–1958

Dutch settlers, or Boers, first arrived in South Africa in the 1650s. They came to believe that the country was theirs by right, and that whites were superior to blacks. By 1948, the Boer government passed a series of laws to allow blacks to be treated differently from whites, with fewer rights. This was called apartheid.

One of its great champions was Johannes Strijdom, a lawyer and politician from Cape Colony. Having helped to set up apartheid, Strijdom became South Africa's prime minister in 1954. He made sure that black Africans were denied equality by making them live in poorer areas, denying them equal opportunities for jobs, and banning them from government. The police force was used to crush any protest demonstrations or strikes by blacks.

▲ Strijdom arrives in London for a Commonwealth conference in 1956. (Nine countries attended; in 1995 there were 53.).

Strijdom was forced to resign in 1957 when he fell seriously ill. The system of apartheid was abolished in 1990, and all the country's different races now have equal rights. South Africa now has a largely black Parliament and a black president, Nelson Mandela.

▼ Under Strijdom's leadership, the system of apartheid was strengthened in South Africa. Separate townships for blacks grew up, such as this one near Johannesburg.

Mao Zedong
1893–1976

'Political power grows out of the barrel of a gun,' wrote Mao Zedong. In 1921, he joined China's Communist Party. China, still a backward country, had got rid of its emperor, but was split by civil war. Mao organized the communist fight against the Nationalist forces in south-eastern China, but by 1934 they were forced to retreat. On the famous 'Long March', he led thousands of followers to safety in north-western China 10,000 km away. From here, he was able to wage war against the Nationalists. The people supported him, and in 1949, Mao became leader of the Republic of China. However, Mao wanted the Communist revolution to continue. In 1958, he planned a 'Great Leap Forward' for China's industry. He ordered peasants to give up their farms and work together on communes. But many of his schemes were failures, and he allowed the police and the People's Army to terrorize anyone who questioned his ideas.

▲ Youthful Red Guards read aloud instructions from the 'Little Red Book' of Mao's thoughts and writings in about 1966. They were Mao's last attempt at continuing the revolution – he sent them out across China to rebel against 'reactionary' government and to destroy anything that was 'old'.

Mao's body can still be seen today. After his death it was preserved, or embalmed, and put on permanent display in the Chinese capital, Beijing.

Robert Menzies
1894–1978

It is hard to think of Robert Menzies as a tyrant. He was a cheerful man, who led Australia for a record total of eighteen years. But he was unpopular with many Australians, because he seemed to have too much power. They nicknamed him 'Ming the Merciless' after the villain in the Flash Gordon comic strip.

In 1928, Menzies began his political career, and he steadily worked his way upwards until, in 1939, he became prime minister. Two years later he was forced to resign after a furious row with his colleagues. But he fought his way back and was elected leader again in 1949. This time he stayed in office for an amazing sixteen years.

Menzies boasted of being 'British to my boot-straps', and annoyed many Australians by supporting the British in their disastrous invasion of Suez in 1956.

He made them even angrier in the 1960s when he sent Australian troops to help the Americans in Vietnam. Menzies was knighted by Queen Elizabeth II in 1963 and resigned from government in 1966.

Menzies hated communism. Perhaps his most tyrannical act was to try to suppress the Australian Communist Party in 1951. The attempt failed.

▶ Prime Minister Menzies leaves the USA for home in 1941. Soon afterwards, he was forced to resign for taking Australia into World War II.

J. Edgar Hoover
1895–1972

Tubby and short, Hoover was for many years the world's most powerful policeman. He served under eight US Presidents. The force he built up was the Federal Bureau of Investigation (the FBI). Hoover was appointed as FBI director in 1924 when it was corrupt and inefficient. Hoover moved fast to smarten it up. He set up training programmes, a fingerprints file and a crime laboratory. His agents hunted down many important criminals and spies.

Hoover insisted on having tight control over all FBI affairs, even to specifying what clothes his agents wore. He also used blackmail, burglary and violence to gain evidence against suspects. He remained as director until his death at the age of 77. His power was so great that no-one dared to remove him.

▲ President Roosevelt signs the bill of 1934 to enforce the fight against gangster crime in the USA, watched by Hoover (directly behind him).

During the 1930s, a wave of violent crime swept the USA. Special FBI agents were trained to deal with it. Nicknamed 'G-Men' (Government Men), they became popular heroes for capturing gangsters, such as John Dillinger and 'Machine Gun' Kelly.

▼ Hoover talks with President John F. Kennedy and his brother Robert, the Attorney General, in 1961.

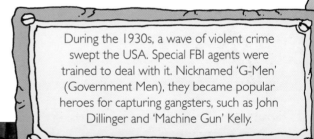

Juan Perón
1895–1974

Juan Perón was popular with his fellow officers in the army. He was also loved by the country's poor, whom he promised to help. But Perón did not rely on popularity. When he ran for the presidency of Argentina in 1946, he sent gangs of thugs to beat up his rivals. As president, he pleased the workers by giving them many benefits, but this angered other Argentinians.

The country's economy also suffered badly. When Perón argued with the Roman Catholic Church in 1955, there were revolts in the armed forces, and he was forced into exile in Spain. However, his followers, the fanatical 'Perónists' remained loyal. In 1973, Perón returned to Argentina. Hugely popular again, he was re-elected as President, but died within a few months.

▲ Supporters of Perón applaud as he casts his vote in the election of 1948. He pleased Argentinians by defying the power of the USA.

Perón's second wife was the glamourous actress, Eva Duarte, who died of cancer in 1952. Her adventures were later celebrated in the hit musical *Evita* by Sir Andrew Lloyd-Webber. In 1974, her corpse was brought back to Argentina and buried in an enormous tomb.

▼ Perón, with his second wife 'Evita', waves to the crowds in Buenos Aires after his re-election in 1952.

Lavrenty Beria
1899–1953

Beria looked and acted like everyone's idea of a secret police chief, being cold-blooded, murderous and cunning. Soon after the Bolsheviks took over in the Russian Revolution of 1917, Beria made a powerful friend in Stalin (see page 71).

When Stalin came to power, he ordered that all anti-revolutionaries should be killed, or purged. Beria was sent to purge the Caucasus region in 1932, and had thousands of people put to death. He even shot one politician in his own office.

In 1938, Beria became head of Stalin's secret police. He now had enormous power, sending many prisoners to slave labour camps, and swiftly murdering anyone even remotely suspected of acting against the state, or treason. He was the most feared man in Russia.

When Stalin died in 1953, Beria attempted to take his place, only to be arrested and shot – for treason. After his death, the Soviet leaders had to explain how such an important man could have been a traitor. They made up a simple story: Beria had been a British spy all along.

▼ Punishment cells at a camp for political prisoners in Siberia, wide open to the freezing wind and snow.

Ngo Dinh Diem
1901–63

By the 1950s, Vietnam had been ruled by France for nearly a century. However, the upheavals of the Second World War had weakened France's control. Her troops struggled with communist independence fighters, called Vietminh. In 1954, the French withdrew and Vietnam was split into two countries: North and South.

The communists controlled North Vietnam, while the South Vietnamese soon grew tired of their Emperor, Bao Dai. In 1955, he was replaced by Ngo Dinh Diem, who had fought against both the French and the communists. Diem was a strong leader, who condemned violence, and so seemed ideal, but he rapidly turned into a hated dictator. His brother was head of the secret police, who silenced all opposition.

Diem thought that the Buddhists were aiding the communists, and had hundreds of them imprisoned or killed. In the end he was assassinated by his own generals.

▲ Ngo Dinh Diem came from a noble Vietnamese family, which had converted to the Roman Catholic faith three centuries before.

In 1965, US troops arrived in Vietnam to help Diem's successor to drive out Communists from the north. After a long and disastrous war, they were forced to withdraw. South Vietnam became Communist in 1975.

▼ Soon after Diem's murder, the USA became more deeply involved in the war between the two Vietnams.

Achmed Sukarno

1901–70

Little Sukarno's playmates in Java called him 'Djago', or 'Champion'. That is what he became. Handsome, charming, ambitious and highly intelligent, he was a brilliant speaker and grew into Indonesia's great revolutionary hero.

By the 1930s, the islands of Indonesia had been under Dutch rule for nearly three centuries. Sukarno joined the movement to fight for independence, and was jailed as a troublemaker.

During the Second World War, the Japanese occupied the islands, and Sukarno allied himself with them. When war ended in 1945, Sukarno became the leader of the country and declared Indonesia to be an independent state. He was proclaimed as president for life in 1963. Despite his ideals, Sukarno was a corrupt and bullying leader, who hated any criticism of his rule. Eventually, he lost the support of the people and was replaced as president in 1968.

Sukarno was fluent in at least ten languages, including Arabic, Dutch, German, Japanese and English, as well as his native Javanese and Indonesian.

▼ Sukarno's corruption and inefficiency helped to plunge Indonesia into growing poverty. Among the poorest were these slum-dwellers, who lived by the railway tracks in Jakarta.

Fulgencio Batista
1901–73

As a boy, Batista saw clearly what a mess Cuba was in. Most people were poor, and society was disrupted by uprisings by black people and poor workers. Batista joined the army and in 1933 organized a 'sergeants' revolt' against the Cuban government. A year later, he took power and became dictator.

Although backed by the army and police, Batista did not rule by terror. He appointed a president to run daily affairs, and also built schools. He felt safe from rebellion, because he had US support. In 1944, he retired to Florida. Almost at once, Cuba was torn by unrest. By 1952, the people were glad to welcome Batista back as president. But now he seemed a harsher man, and took severe measures, abolishing press freedom and forcing the government to carry out his wishes.

▲ Che Guevara, the revolutionary and guerrilla leader, helped Castro to oust Batista. He was later executed while trying to spread Communist revolution in South America.

▼ Batista and his wife in Miami, Florida. They spent eight years there before returning to Cuba in 1952.

In 1958, Batista was forced into exile by a communist revolt led by Fidel Castro. The US government, who had been friendly with Batista, tried hard to get rid of Castro. In 1961, they landed an army of Cuban exiles on the island at the Bay of Pigs. This attempted invasion was a disaster, easily crushed by Castro.

Reinhard Heydrich
1904–42

Of all of Hitler's Nazi henchmen, Heydrich was one of the most savage and sinister. Forced to leave the navy in 1931, his first post was with the Munich police force, where he controlled Dachau, a concentration camp.

In 1938, he masterminded a week of violence against German Jews. He then became deputy to the dreaded Heinrich Himmler, head of the Nazi secret police, the organization known as the SS. When war came, Heydrich formed special SS companies whose job was to exterminate Jews and gypsies as the German armies advanced across Europe.

In 1941, he was made Protector of Bohemia and Moravia. His 'protection' consisted of executing 300 Czechs soon after he arrived, and establishing a rule of terror. Heydrich was so hated that he was called 'The Hangman'.

In May 1942, four Czech resistance fighters were sent from Britain with one aim: to kill The Hangman. As Heydrich was driven by, they shot him and hurled a grenade. Terribly wounded, he died eight days later in agony.

The Nazis took a terrible revenge for Heydrich's assassination. Two mining villages near the Czech city of Prague were destroyed and over 200 inhabitants killed.

▶ Heydrich was a dedicated sportsman. He is shown here in his role as Leader of the Fencing Section of the Nazi Sport Movement.

Hastings Banda
born 1902

Banda was born in the African country then called Nyasaland. As a child he worked in the gold mines, but later he travelled to the USA and then Britain where he qualified as a doctor. While he was away, Nyasaland was joined into a federation with white-dominated Rhodesia (now called Zimbabwe).

Banda was angry at this, and returned home to lead protests against the federation. He was imprisoned, but later released to become prime minister when Nyasaland became independent in 1964 under its new name, Malawi. Banda immediately established firm control of the government. He abolished rival political parties, and forced several of his ministers to resign. All opponents were imprisoned or executed. He was only ousted by a legal election in 1994.

▲ Banda at a London press conference in 1968. He was then not only President, but also Prime Minister, Foreign Minister and Justice Minister!

▼ Banda became Prime Minister of the newly independent Malawi in 1964. Soon afterwards, several colleagues resigned in protest at his dictatorial ways.

Malawi is a very beautiful country with a huge lake running down its eastern side. In fact, the name Malawi means 'the lake where the sun's haze is reflected in the water like fire'.

François Duvalier
1907–71

Doctor Duvalier, or 'Papa Doc', seemed a dedicated and idealistic man. He worked hard to prevent the spread of malaria and other diseases in the Caribbean island of Haiti. In 1949, he was appointed minister of health and opposed the military government. He was elected president of Haiti in 1957, and promised reforms.

Once in power Duvalier showed himself to be ruthless and cruel. He did not trust the army, so he raised his own ruthless force, called the Tontons Macoutes, or 'Bogeymen'. They beat up or killed Duvalier's opponents, and terrorized ordinary Haitians. Other countries, alarmed by his tyrannical rule, turned against Haiti. But Duvalier somehow stayed in command, turning himself into an almost god-like figure through voodoo.

▲ Papa Doc Duvalier with his portly son and successor Jean-Claude, or Baby Doc, who became President at the age of 20.

▼ Some of the dreaded Tontons Macoutes, Duvalier's private army.

Duvalier was still president of Haiti when he died. Even after death, Haiti's nightmare went on. Duvalier named his son Jean-Claude (nicknamed 'Baby Doc') to succeed him. However, Baby Doc was not as strong as his father and by 1986 his authority had collapsed and he fled the country.

Enver Hoxha
1908–85

In 1939, Albania was invaded by Italian troops and a new tobacco store opened in Tirana, the capital. It was run by an ex-teacher named Enver Hoxha, who was a communist and hated the Italians. It soon became the meeting place for local communists. When Albania was freed in 1944, Hoxha became prime minister. Within a decade, he had also put himself in charge of the armed forces and foreign policy.

Hoxha forced his backward country to develop fast. He herded workers on to farms, and built factories and power stations. His methods were brutal: private property was seized by the state, all churches and mosques were closed, and everyone who resisted was exiled, imprisoned or shot.

▲ Hoxha remained the unopposed ruler of Albania for an incredible forty years.

▼ Under Hoxha, farmland was taken from landowners and made into large plots, worked collectively by local people. This allowed Albania to grow enough food to feed itself.

While Hoxha was in power, Albania remained shut off from the rest of the world. Communist rule there collapsed soon after Hoxha's death. Hoxha was not the only reason for Albania's isolation. It is a rugged country, with mountains on three sides making it very difficult to enter. The fourth side, on the Adriatic, is only a short boat ride from the popular Greek island, Corfu.

Kwame Nkrumah
1909–72

Kwame Nkrumah had one ambition – he passionately wanted to see all African nations become free and independent. His own country, the Gold Coast (now Ghana), had been under British control for over a century.

Nkrumah learned about politics while being educated in the USA and England. When he returned home in 1947, he encouraged the people to riot against the British. This won him a year in prison, but in 1952 he became the Gold Coast's prime minister. Five years later, the new state of Ghana became independent, with Nkrumah as its leader.

He used his growing power to help other African countries towards independence. Unfortunately, he would not tolerate any opposition - most of all in Ghana itself. Many people were imprisoned without trial, and rival political parties were banned. Several attempts were made to kill Nkrumah. Then, when he was out of the country in 1966, the armed forces seized power.

Ghana took its name in 1957 from an ancient African empire, but this had existed in another part of the continent. The first Empire of Ghana, which flourished about a thousand years ago, covered parts of modern Mali and Mauritania.

▶ During riots in Ghana in 1948, Nkrumah had been arrested by the British. By 1960, as his country's leader, he was an honoured guest in London, as shown here.

Joseph McCarthy
1908–57

Nobody thought much of Senator Joe McCarthy from Wisconsin, USA. He was not very intelligent, and had coarse manners, swearing and belching without apology. Then, in February 1950, McCarthy stunned the US government by announcing that 205 people in the State Department were communist supporters.

Suddenly, he was headline news – even though he was unable to produce any hard evidence. Many Americans at that time were scared of a communist threat from the USSR and China. It was easy for them to believe that communist agents were trying to take over the government. McCarthy played on these fears in order to gain power in the Senate.

In 1953, he became chairman of a special committee to investigate the so-called communist plotters. This became a frenzied crusade, in which writers, actors and many other famous people were questioned and insulted. Finally, McCarthy went too far and attacked President Eisenhower himself. He was stripped of his powers and died largely forgotten.

▼ Using a huge map of the USA, McCarthy points out centres of Communist Party organization. Next to him, looking understandably fed-up, is one of his opponents.

Ironically enough, McCarthy did himself most harm by appearing on television. A live showing of his grilling of suspected army officers in 1954 demonstrated just what a crude bully he was, and his popularity quickly declined.

Alfredo Stroessner
born 1912

Between 1870 and 1954, Paraguay had more than forty presidents. Between 1954 and 1989, it had only one. His name was Alfredo Stroessner, the son of a German settler. He became an officer at the age of 20. Ambitious and ruthless, in 1951 he rose to become commander of Paraguay's armed forces.

The country had been split by civil war and rebellion for many years. In 1954, Stroessner seized power and brought peace and stability – by force. His government modernized Paraguay by building roads and schools and encouraging new farming methods. But it was at the cost of personal freedom.

▲ Adolf Eichmann, the Nazi, on trial in Israel in 1961. Many Nazis took refuge in Paraguay after 1945.

Paraguay partly owns (with Brazil) the biggest power-station in the world, at the Itaipu dam on the Paraná River. But in building the dam, the country lost its greatest tourist attraction – the Guaira Falls, once the world's largest waterfall.

All opponents were either imprisoned or sent abroad. After winning eight consecutive uncontested elections, he was eventually removed from office by an army rebellion.

▼ Stroessner forged strong links with another harsh regime, that of South Africa. Here, (second left) he meets the South African President Fouchs (left).

Kim Il-Sung
1912–94

At the end of the Second World War, Korea was split into two. The South was supported by the USA, while the North became a communist state, supported by Russia. From 1948, the leader of North Korea was Kim Il-Sung, a communist who had fought bravely against Japan.

Kim wanted his country to be united again. In 1950, he led North Korean troops in an attack on the South. This war (called the Korean War) lasted until 1953 and ended in stalemate. However, it gave Kim the chance to strengthen his power at home. He got rid of all rivals and governed as a dictator.

Kim was a severe and arrogant ruler. He forced the North Koreans to train in army units and to work on farms. He also glorified himself, ordering that he should be called the 'Great Leader', and huge monuments and portraits be displayed in his honour. After his death, he was succeeded by his son, Kim Chong Il, the 'Dear Leader'.

▼ After Kim's death, millions of North Koreans mourned the loss of the 'Father of the Nation'.

Kim's real name was Kim Song Ju. He changed it during the 1930s when he was being trained as a soldier in Russia, taking the name of a famous Korean freedom fighter against the Japanese.

Jiang Qing
1914–91

Many Chinese communists were shocked when their leader, Mao Zedong, decided to marry an actress. She was much younger than him and, worst of all, Mao was already married. However, the marriage went ahead, on condition that Jiang Qing kept out of politics.

She kept her promise until the Cultural Revolution in the 1960s. This radical movement aimed at reforming the country's revolutionary government. In fact, it turned into a fanatical crusade against writers, artists, teachers and anyone who could be accused of being a 'class enemy'. Jiang quickly became a leader of the Cultural Revolution. In wild speeches, she encouraged the young Red Guards to attack and destroy all evidence of China's traditional culture. After Mao's death, she gradually lost power. Put on trial for causing civil unrest, she was condemned to life imprisonment.

▲ Mao with his third wife Jiang Qing.

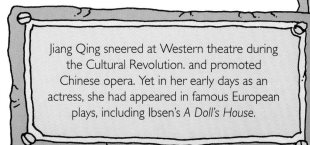

Jiang Qing sneered at Western theatre during the Cultural Revolution. and promoted Chinese opera. Yet in her early days as an actress, she had appeared in famous European plays, including Ibsen's *A Doll's House*.

▼ Jiang Qing goes on trial in 1980.

Augusto Pinochet
born 1915

In 1970, the people of Chile elected their first communist president, Salvator Allende. He tried to make life fairer for the poor, dividing up large farms and taking control of the copper mines for the state. But many were alarmed at his communist ideas. After three years, Allende was overthrown and killed.

He was followed by Augusto Pinochet – a harsh soldier, commander of Chile's armed forces. He was named president, and immediately set out to crush all opposition in a reign of terror. More than 130,000 people were arrested, and one million fled the country.

Pinochet also reversed Allende's policies. He seized farmland from the peasants and gave it back to its original owners. He dissolved Chile's Parliament and banned rival political parties. But eventually, in 1988, he allowed free elections. Most people voted against him, and he handed over power two years later.

Many people believe that the CIA (the USA's spy service) helped Pinochet to overthrow Allende. They were worried at having a Communist state in South America.

▼ In 1984, over 3, 000 shanty dwellers were rounded up and moved to a football stadium to be questioned. Two secret agents stand in the centre.

Ferdinand Marcos
1917–89

'This nation can be great again,' promised Ferdinand Marcos in 1965. He had just been elected president of the Philippines. At first, he seemed to be keeping his promise – new roads and schools were built, and rice farmers were helped to increase their crops. Marcos was re-elected in 1969. By now, the magic had faded. Peasants demanded more land, students protested against corruption, and terrorists exploded a bomb in the capital, Manila.

In 1972, Marcos imposed martial law in the Philippines. Then he announced that he would continue as president as long as he wanted, without an election. Growing steadily more tyrannical, he gave well-paid jobs to his family (notably his wife, Imelda), and stole a huge sum of money from the state. His downfall began when his main opponent, Benazon Aquino, was murdered. Many thought Marcos had ordered the killing, and unrest increased. Early in 1986, Marcos and his wife fled into exile.

▼ Thousands of Filipinos surround the tanks sent to arrest Marcos's opponents in 1986 and bring them to a halt. Two days later, Marcos fled.

Imelda Marcos was famous for her greed and extravagance. When crowds broke into the Marcos' palace, they found she had left 3,000 pairs of shoes. She has recently made something of a comeback in Filipino politics, being elected as a senator in 1995.

Nicolae Ceausescu
1918–89

At the age of 18, Ceausescu was already a committed member of Romania's Communist Party. He was imprisoned twice for his activities. The second time, he shared a cell with Gheorge Gheorghiu-Dej, and they became close friends. When the communists came to power in 1945, Gheorghiu-Dej was leader, and made Ceausescu his deputy.

In 1965, after his friend's death, Ceausescu rose to be party leader, and then president. His government proved to be a disaster. He started grand but ridiculous schemes. In one, he sold most of the country's food supply to pay off foreign debts – the result was a famine.

Ceausescu allowed no-one to question his authority. His secret police arrested and killed many people. His family held important posts in government and were notoriously corrupt.

▲ Ceausescu ordered the destruction of many ancient Romanian villages to make way for new apartment blocks such as this.

After riots in 1989, his tyranny collapsed and, following a summary trial, he and Elena were shot by a firing squad. Four days after Ceausescu's execution, Romania ceased to be a communist state. Within five months, the first free elections for over fifty years were held.

▼ Ceausescu with his wife Elena. She wielded almost as much political power as her husband, and was Deputy Prime Minister.

Jean Bedel Bokassa
born 1921

Bokassa had one of the strangest careers of all dictators. Born in French Equatorial Africa (now part of the Central African Republic), he became a distinguished soldier in France's colonial army, winning medals and the rank of captain. When the Central African Republic was formed in 1960, Bokassa returned home to head the armed forces. By 1966, he had ousted the Republic's leader and made himself president.

A reign of terror began, and Bokassa took all important government posts for himself. In 1977, he declared himself emperor, and crowned himself on a golden throne. The ceremony cost US$200 million, nearly bankrupting his country.

Bokassa's savagery was startling. In 1979, he arrested hundreds of schoolchildren for refusing to wear uniforms (which were made in a factory he owned). At least a hundred children were murdered by his imperial guard. This was too much for the French government: its troops were sent to help overthrow Bokassa, who fled into exile.

▲ Bokassa is crowned Emperor of the Central African Republic in a magnificent, but very wasteful, ceremony in 1977.

The strangest episode of all came seven years after Bokassa fled into exile. He returned to the C.A.R. of his own free will in 1986. He was immediately sentenced to life imprisonment, and was locked up in solitary confinement.

▼ The deposed Emperor (left) goes on trial after his return to Africa in 1986.

Robert Maxwell

1923–92

Robert Maxwell started life as Ludvik Hoch in Czechoslovakia. During the Second World War, he fought so bravely for the British army that he won the Military Cross. In 1944, he promised his new wife: 'I shall make my fortune. I shall be prime minister of England'.

Maxwell never led his adopted country, Britain. But he did become one of the most powerful newspaper owners in the world. He also ran book publishers, film companies and football clubs. Many disliked him for his brutal way with his employees. They might be sacked without notice, bullied, shouted at or humiliated. But Maxwell was respected for his spectacular business success.

Then, out of the blue, came shock news. Maxwell was found drowned near his luxury yacht. Immediately, many of

▲ Maxwell prided himself on his contacts with Communist countries. Here, he presents books to Leonid Brezhnev, leader of the Soviet Union, in 1978.

his companies were revealed to be in deep financial trouble. Worst of all, the huge pension fund built up for the benefit of Mirror Group workers had simply disappeared. Maxwell had used its assets for his business dealings.

▼ Robert Maxwell at the launch of his newspaper *The European* in 1990.

Maxwell's piratical way of buying up companies made some people distrust him. They called him 'The Bouncing Czech', because they believed he had no money in the bank to back up his purchases.

Idi Amin
born 1924

'I myself consider myself ... to be the most important figure in the world' said Idi Amin in a radio interview in 1976. He had then been dictator of Uganda for five years, and was one of the most feared (and laughed-at) leaders in the world.

Amin was born into one of Uganda's smallest tribes, and trained as a soldier in the British army. After Uganda became independent from Britain in 1962, he commanded the armed forces. In 1971, he seized power and declared himself head of state. Amin's sudden mood swings, from smiles to savagery, terrified most Ugandans. He ordered the torture and murder of up to 300,000 people from the larger tribes. He insulted the USA, Britain and Israel, as well as African states. In 1979, Uganda was invaded by Tanzania, and Amin fled into exile.

▲ Amin, nicknamed 'Big Daddy', greatly enjoyed uniforms, his many medals and ceremonial. Here he is presiding at a degree ceremony in Kampala.

▼ Amin was popular with other African rulers. Here he is entertaining President Tolbert of Liberia.

One of Amin's stupidest acts was to expel all Asians from Uganda. They mostly were from the Indian sub-continent and were the country's most successful businessmen. With their departure, Uganda's economy collapsed.

Pol Pot
born 1928

Pol Pot is renowned as one of the most bloodthirsty tyrants of the twentieth century. Yet he spent two years as a Buddhist monk, and later worked as a teacher. All this time, he was a member of the Cambodian Communist Party, working to take power in Cambodia.

The country had become involved in the Vietnam War, and US troops had crossed the border to hunt down communists. Pol Pot took advantage of this turmoil, and launched an attack on the government with his ferocious guerrilla army, the Khmer Rouge. By 1975, they had seized control of Cambodia, which they renamed Kampuchea.

Pol Pot and his colleagues now began their murderous reign. Everyone was forced to dress alike. Townspeople were sent to work as peasants. All educated

▲ Pol Pot in his secret hideout during the Vietnamese invasion of Cambodia in 1979. He boasted that his guerrillas were 'spread out across the nation like the mesh of a net'.

Some of the bloodshed of Pol Pot's years in power was portrayed in the successful US film, *The Killing Fields*, which was released in 1988.

people were rounded up, and sent to forced labour camps or killed. Hundreds of thousands fled into exile in Thailand.

Within five years, over 1,000,000 Cambodians died from torture, starvation or execution. In 1979, Vietnamese troops invaded Cambodia and drove out Pol Pot, but he still led the Khmer Rouge. The Khmer Rouge are still fighting the new government of Kampuchea and taxing the people in areas where they operate.

◄ One of the hundreds of mass graves discovered in Kampuchea after the Khmer Rouge were expelled.

James Jones
1931–78

James 'Jim' Jones was born in Indiana, USA, where he became an evangelical preacher. In 1955, he set up his own church: The Peoples Temple Full Gospel Church. It mixed blacks and whites in the congregation – extremely unusual then.

In 1964 he and his flock moved to California. Jones now refused to accept the Bible and claimed he was Jesus Christ reborn. Slowly the Temples became more secretive and introduced strange and bizarre rituals over the next ten years.

The colony at Jonestown in Guyana was started in 1974 as a refuge from world war. Following media exposés of the Temples as a cult, all Jones's followers had moved there by late 1977. Jones lied to his people about events in the USA and made them practice a rite of mass suicide on what he called 'white nights'.

▲ The Reverend 'Jim' Jones preaching and giving the black power salute, possibly in 1972. This photo was found in an album at Jonestown after the tragedy.

▼ This was the appalling sight at the Peoples Temple in Jonestown on 20 November 1978.

On 18 November 1978, Congressman Leo Ryan, some of a group called Concerned Relatives and some reporters visited Jonestown. As they left they were ambushed and five people, including Ryan were murdered. Jones announced his final 'white night', brewed a batch of poison and 914 people, including little children, died. Only four survived – three fled and one was forgotten.

Saddam Hussein
born 1937

As a young man, Saddam joined the Ba'ath Socialist Party. This movement is in many parts of the Arab world and is devoted to 'freedom, unity and socialism'. However, Saddam has done little to promote these ideals in Iraq.

Saddam twice had to flee from Iraq, wounded and hunted as a political enemy. But by 1968, his party was in power, and in 1979 he was president. Iraq became a police state, with many opponents to Saddam being imprisoned without trial and tortured. Saddam's foreign policy was even more aggressive. In 1980, his troops invaded Iran in a wasteful attempt to capture its oil fields. In 1990, he overran Kuwait. This action horrified the world, and many countries sent troops to drive him out. Saddam's army was crushed, but somehow he managed to cling on to power.

▲ Black smoke pours from blazing Kuwaiti oil wells, set light by Iraqi troops as they retreated during the Gulf War of 1991.

▼ Saddam runs a huge personality cult in Iraq.

Saddam tried to drive out the homeless Kurds who had settled in northern Iraq, murdering a whole village with poison gas. Since 1990, over 900,000 Kurds have fled as refugees into neighbouring Turkey and Iran. He also attacked the Marsh Arabs who live along the Euphrates.

Kate 'Ma' Barker
1872–1935

Kate Barker must have been a very strange child in nineteenth century America. Her heroes were all villains – ruthless criminals and gangsters! She taught her four sons to be villains too, planning bank raids for them. She beat them up if they didn't hand over her share of the spoils. Not surprisingly, all four grew up to be vicious killers.

By the late 1920s, three of her sons were in jail and the fourth was dead (he shot himself when cornered by the police). Kate fought hard to get her sons released. When two, Freddie and Arthur were freed, the Barker gang began kidnapping rich people and demanding huge ransoms for them.

The police had no idea where their hideout was until they captured Arthur in Chicago in 1935. In his home, they found a map showing exactly where the gang was hiding. Police surrounded the house in Florida and, after a ferocious gun battle, 'Ma' and Freddie were killed.

Kidnapping was a widespread crime in the USA in the 1920s and 1930s. In 1932, the baby son of Charles Lindbergh, the first pilot to fly the Atlantic solo, was kidnapped and murdered. This led to the so-called 'Lindbergh Law', which made it a federal crime to take a victim across a state line or to use the US postal services for ransom demands.

▼ The bodies of Freddie Barker and his mother, 'Ma' Barker, in the morgue of Oklavaha, Florida, in 1935.

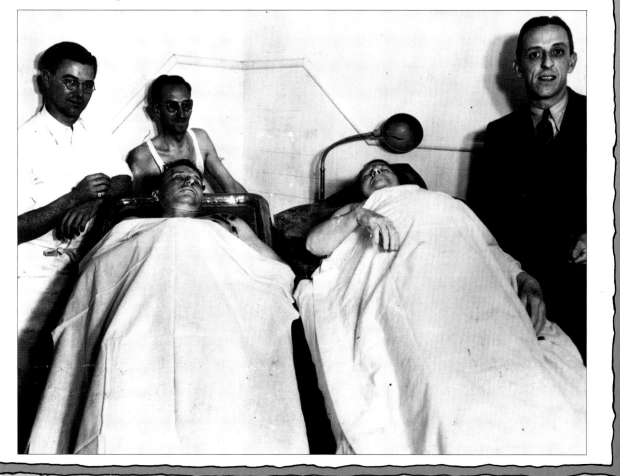

Samuel Doe
1950–90

The state of Liberia, on Africa's west coast, was originally a home for freed slaves from the USA. During the nineteenth century, thousands of black settlers crossed the Atlantic. They were joined by many other native Africans. But it was the US families who took control of the new land.

By 1980, the native Africans were angry at the power and wealth of the Americans. Led by a young army sergeant called Samuel Doe, a group of military men attacked the president's house. They killed the president, then tried and executed his main supporters. Doe, until then almost unknown, became the new leader.

▲ Doe was only a Master Sergeant in the Liberian army when he seized power. He appointed other low-ranking officers to assist him.

The name Liberia comes from the Latin word for freedom, or free land. The state was founded in 1822, with the support of US President James Monroe. The capital city of Monrovia was named in his honour.

Doe immediately promoted himself to general. He gave important posts to members of his own tribe. In 1985, he held elections, and announced that his party had won.

Many people, however, believed that the results were rigged. There was great unrest, and Doe removed all opposition with great savagery. In 1990 a rebel army attacked the capital, Monrovia, and killed him. The extremely bloody civil war that followed between three competing armies, lasted for two years and ruined the country and its economy.

◀ Liberian troops play with the skull of a rebel soldier.

David Koresh
1959–93

Vernon Wayne Howell was a misfit. Skinny, backward and trouble-making, he found it hard to make friends. He was thrown out of his church for pestering the pastor's daughter. Howell next joined the Branch Davidians, an obscure religious cult based near the town of Waco in Texas, USA.

Even here, he made enemies. After a fierce argument, he left to set up another Davidian community nearby. Over fifty followers joined him, obedient to his every word. His behaviour became increasingly strange. He declared that he was a second Christ, and allowed to have 140 wives. Certainly, he had dozens of mistresses, many of them as young as 12 years old.

▲ Vernon Howell, looking relaxed and confident in his new character as David Koresh, the Son of God.

Koresh only allowed his followers to watch three films - over and over again. They were all violent war movies: *Hamburger Hill*, *Platoon* and *Full Metal Jacket*.

In 1987, Howell moved back to the Branch Davidian headquarters at Waco. But the police had grown suspicious of the cult. Howell (now calling himself David Koresh) began to prepare for a siege, buying guns and explosives.

Following a fifty-one day siege after being refused access by the cultists, federal agents attacked the headquarters on 19 April 1993. During the fight that followed, the buildings went up in flames. Seventy-two bodies were found, including that of David Koresh. It is believed that most of them had committed suicide as the fire started.

◀ The Mount Carmel complex of the Branch Davidians at Waco burning down.

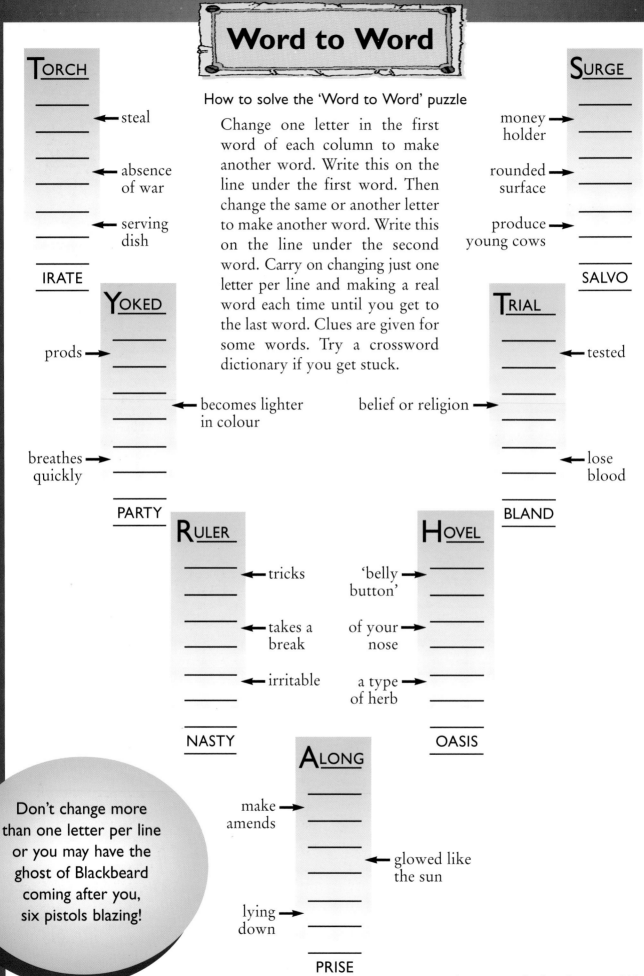

Word to Word

How to solve the 'Word to Word' puzzle

Change one letter in the first word of each column to make another word. Write this on the line under the first word. Then change the same or another letter to make another word. Write this on the line under the second word. Carry on changing just one letter per line and making a real word each time until you get to the last word. Clues are given for some words. Try a crossword dictionary if you get stuck.

TORCH

← steal

← absence of war

← serving dish

IRATE

YOKED

prods →

← becomes lighter in colour

breathes quickly →

PARTY

SURGE

money holder →

rounded surface →

produce young cows →

SALVO

TRIAL

← tested

belief or religion →

← lose blood

BLAND

RULER

← tricks

← takes a break

← irritable

NASTY

HOVEL

'belly button' →

of your nose →

a type of herb →

OASIS

ALONG

make amends →

← glowed like the sun

lying down →

PRISE

Don't change more than one letter per line or you may have the ghost of Blackbeard coming after you, six pistols blazing!

Answers can be found on page 111

108

Index

Picture Acknowledgements

a = above, b = below

AKG, London: 20b, 33a.
Bridgeman Art Library:
Barber's Hall, London 34b;
Bibliotheque de Prostantisme,
Paris/ Giraudon 33b;
Bibliotheque Nationale, Paris
22, 25a; British Library, London
21b, 24a & b; Entoven
Collection, London 19b;
Kunsthistorisches Museum,
Vienna 15b, 30a; Louvre, Paris
15a; Louvre, Paris/ Giraudon
51b; Musée Condé, Chantilly
13a; Musée de la Ville de Paris,
Musée Carnavalet/ Giraudon
50b; Musée des Beaux-Arts,
Chartres/ Giraudon 47b;
National Museum of India,
New Delhi 40b; Novosti 36b;
Palacio Nacional, Mexico 29,
57b; Powis Castle, Wales 48a;
Private Collections 11a, 14a, 6

& 16a, 36a, 41a, 45b, 46b, 57a;
Richardson and Kailas Icons,
London 23; Sean Sprague/
Mexicolore 53; Staatliche
Schlosser und Garten, Potsdam
43b; Syon House, Middlesex
32a; Tretiakov Gallery, Moscow
38a; Vatican Museums and
Galleries, Rome 18b; Victoria
and Albert Museum, London
31b, 7 & 48b; Wallace
Collection, London 32b.
CameraPress: 105a, Mohamed
Ansar 103a; Rodney Bond 55b;
Peter Goodwin 70a; Marion
Kaplan 101a; Jan Kopez 93b;
Juan Pablo, Lira/Doce 94a, 94b,
95b, 96a; R. Mildenhall 90a,
90b; P. O'Donnell 99a 100b;
Gerry Pinches 102b; David
Rubinger 98b; Blair Seitz 97a;
Fernando Sosa 62b; Terence
Spencer 79a, 79b, 84a, 85a.
Mary Evans Picture Library:
8a, 7 &18a, 25b, 27, 28a, 33a,
34a, 40a, 42, 43a, 44a, 49, 51a,
55a, 6 & 63a, 64a, 64b, 1 & 71a,
72a, 72b, 73a, 77a.
Ronald Grant Archive: 67b.
Robert Harding Picture

Library: 101b; Nigel Blythe
37b; FPG International 73b;
Tony Waltham 12.
**Hulton Deutsch Collection
Ltd:** 8b, 11b, 13b, 14b, 17a &b,
18b, 21a, 26a & b, 28b, 31a, 38b,
39b, 54a, 56a, 58a, 58b, 61, 62a,
68, 69a & b, 70b, 76b, 78a, 81b,
91a. **Hutchison Library:** John
G. Egan 98a; Sarah Errington
85b, 89b; J. G. Fuller 54b; Gail
Goodger 41b; Maurice Harvey
68b; N. Haslem 30b; R. Lloyd
78b; Oleg Parshin 71b, 83b.
**Illustrated London News
Picture Library:** 46a, 59a, 59b,
63b. **Image Select:** 39a, 60.
Mansell Collection: 19a, 50a.
National Maritime Museum:
45a, 52.
Novosti: 47a.
Popperfoto: 74, 75a, 75b, 76a,
82b, 83a, 84b, 86a, 86b, 87, 88a,
88b, 93a, 96b, 97b, 99b, 102a,
105b, 107a.
Corbis-Bettmann Archive:
56b, 66a, 66b, 77b, 106a, 106b,
107b; Reuters 103b; UPI 67a,
80, 81a, 82a, 89a, 92, 6 & 95a,
100a, 104. **Royal Geographical**

Society: 65a. **Ronald
Sheridan/Ancient Art and
Architecture Collection:** 9, 10a,
10b, 20a, 33b, 37a, 44b.

COVER CREDITS
Front, clockwise from top left:
Mary Evans Picture Library,
Bridgeman Art Library (Musée
des Beaux-Arts, Chartres/
Giraudon), Mary Evans Picture
Library and the following four,
Bridgeman Art Library
(Kunsthistorisches Museum,
Vienna), Bridgeman Art Library
(Barbers' Hall, London), Mary
Evans Picture Library,
Bridgeman Art Library
(Louvre, Paris), Image Select.
Back, clockwise from top left:
Hulton Deutsch, Bridgeman
Art Library (Private
Collection), Hulton Deutsch,
Hulton Deutsch, Camera Press,
Camera Press, Hulton Deutsch,
Bridgeman Art Library (Private
Collection), Bridgeman Art
Library (Victoria & Albert
Museum, London), Hulton
Deutsch.